Daily Estimation Adventure

Grade 6

 McGraw Hill Children's Publishing

Abbreviations Used in This Book

English system *(note periods)*

Length	Area	Volume	Weight	Capacity
inch(es). in. or "	square inch(es). sq. in.	cubic inch(es). cu. in. or in.³	ounce(s). oz.	pint(s). pt.
foot (feet). ft. or '	square foot (feet). sq. ft.	cubic foot (feet). cu. ft. or ft.³	pound(s). lb.	quart(s). qt.
yard(s). yd.	square yard(s). sq. yd.	cubic yard(s). cu. yd. or yd.³		
mile(s) mi.	square mile(s). sq. mi.			

Metric and International system *(note no periods)*

Length	Area	Volume	Weight	Capacity
centimeter(s). cm	square centimeter(s). sq cm	cubic centimeter(s). cm³	gram(s). g	milliliters(s). mL
meter(s). m	square meter(s). sq m	cubic meter(s). cu m	kilogram(s). kg	liter(s). L
kilometer(s). km	square kilometer(s). sq km			

Other

Time *(note plural forms)*	Temperature	Other
second(s). sec. (secs.)	Fahrenheit. F	miles per gallon. mpg
minute(s). min. (mins.)	Celsius. C	miles per hour. mph
hour(s). hr. (hrs.)		approximately equals. ≈
month(s). mo. (mos.)		circumference. C
year(s). yr. (yrs.)		perimeter. P

Author: Margaret Thomas

Children's Publishing

Published by McGraw-Hill
An imprint of McGraw-Hill Children's Publishing
Copyright © 2004 McGraw-Hill Children's Publishing

All Rights Reserved • Printed in the United States of America

Limited Reproduction Permission: Permission to duplicate these materials is limited to the person for whom they are purchased. Reproduction for an entire school or school district is unlawful and strictly prohibited.

Send all inquiries to:
McGraw-Hill Children's Publishing
3195 Wilson Drive NW
Grand Rapids, Michigan 49544

Daily Estimation Adventure—grade 6
ISBN: 0-7696-3416-8

1 2 3 4 5 6 7 8 9 MAL 09 08 07 06 05 04

Contents

Standards Correlation Chart 3
Introduction. 4
Estimation Activities. 5
Answer Key. 77

Standards Correlation Chart

NCTM Content Standards	Problems
Number and Operations (N)	1, 2, 3, 4, 5, 6, 7, 8, 9, 10, 11, 12, 13, 15, 16, 17, 21, 23, 25, 26, 27, 29, 31, 32, 33, 34, 35, 36, 37, 39, 40, 42, 45, 46, 47, 54, 56, 59, 60, 61, 62, 63, 64, 65, 66, 68, 70, 72, 73, 74, 75, 76, 78, 79, 80, 83, 87, 88, 90, 91, 92, 94, 96, 97, 98, 99, 101, 102, 103, 105, 107, 109, 112, 113, 114, 116, 118, 119, 121, 123, 125, 127, 132, 135, 139, 142, 144, 145, 148, 150, 151, 153, 154, 155, 156, 158, 159, 163, 164, 165, 166, 167, 169, 170, 171, 172, 173, 175, 178, 180
Algebra (A)	6, 7, 8, 34, 46, 57, 59, 61, 69, 87, 89, 97, 98, 107, 110, 123, 125, 134, 135, 137, 138, 146, 147, 148, 157, 160
Geometry (G)	18, 19, 30, 38, 42, 44, 47, 49, 50, 64, 71, 81, 85, 100, 115, 130, 131, 149, 151, 152, 161, 174, 176
Measurement (M)	8, 14, 18, 19, 20, 22, 28, 38, 39, 41, 43, 49, 50, 51, 52, 53, 54, 55, 58, 69, 71, 77, 83, 84, 85, 86, 89, 91, 93, 95, 100, 108, 115, 120, 122, 124, 126, 127, 128, 129, 130, 131, 133, 136, 137, 138, 140, 141, 142, 143, 144, 145, 149, 152, 161, 162, 168, 174, 175, 176, 177
Data Analysis and Probability (D)	2, 24, 67, 82, 103, 104, 106, 111, 114, 117, 118, 119, 121, 126, 139, 140, 168, 179

© McGraw-Hill Children's Publishing

0-7696-3416-8 *Daily Estimation Adventure*

Introduction

Daily Estimation Adventure is based on the most recent content standards from the National Council of Teachers of Mathematics (NCTM). The series supports programs that enable students to master the standards in each content area. In *Daily Estimation Adventure*—grade 6, for your convenience, each activity is labeled with the standard(s) it meets. The content-area standards are (with identifying labels used in this book):

Number and Operations (N)
Algebra (A)
Geometry (G)
Measurement (M)
Data Analysis and Probability (D)

Making "reasonable estimates" is a skill specifically mentioned in the NCTM standards for number and operations.

In many life situations, using estimates is preferable to figuring exact answers. Estimations are not mere guesses but conclusions based on previous knowledge and a person's ability to project beyond what she or he sees. Estimating requires well-developed skills in reading, in judging reasonableness of answers, and in critical thinking. In grade 6, *Daily Estimation Adventure* will help students develop numbers concepts and skills as well as spatial sense.

You may want to work with your class as a whole to complete the activities in *Daily Estimation Adventure*, use small or paired groups, or assign the activities as individual work. Some activities are more adaptable to one method or another. You may wish to use an overhead projector or to cut apart the activities on the pages and place them in an estimation center for individual work.

Whichever format you choose for presenting the activities, encourage students to think about why they are estimating, how they estimated, and if an estimate or an exact answer is the best solution for each problem.

Lunch for Four   1

Carmen has $15. Is that enough for lunch for 4 people if each person has a taco, an order of nachos, and a drink?
(Hint: Round the prices to the nearest dollar.)

Menu	
Taco	89¢
Burrito	$1.09
Nachos	99¢
Drink	79¢
Crisp-its	69¢

Game Tickets   2

Category	Price
A	$15.95
B	$11.95
C	$7.95

Compatible numbers are numbers that are easily computed.

Example: $\frac{26}{9} \approx \frac{27}{9}$ or 3

Use compatible numbers to answer the following.

1. If Jackie has $32.78, how many C-category game tickets can she buy?
2. If Alice has $50.17, how many B-category game tickets can she buy?
3. Jackie and Alice decide to combine their money. How many A-category game tickets can they buy?

3 Quick Estimate—
Whole Numbers I

1. Which is the best estimate for 38 x 45?
    a. 170   b. 1710   c. 17710

2. Which is the best estimate for 8217 ÷ 99?
    a. 0.83   b. 8.3   c. 83

4 Missing Points

Each multiplication problem is missing the decimal point in the product. Locate the decimal point in each product. Insert zeros if needed.

1. 2.2 x .011 242	**2.** 55 x 0.033 1815	**3.** 0.05 x 0.11 55	**4.** 0.6 x 1.7 102
5. 12.8 x 0.12 1536	**6.** 6.9 x 11 759	**7.** 66.2 x 1.1 7282	**8.** 32.1 x 2.02 64842
9. 1.8 x 6.03 10854	**10.** 6.7 x 0.801 53667	**11.** 0.84 x 0.07 588	**12.** 8.2 x 0.1 82

Line Up 5

Locate each point on the number line.

A $\frac{2}{3}$; B 0.09; C $\frac{1}{3}$; D $\frac{1}{5}$; E 0.25

```
|_____|_____|
0                   1                   1
                    2
```

Amusement Park I 6

The Robert's Rides park charges $9.99/student or child and $14.99/adult admission. Give a reasonable estimate for the total admission charge for your class and three chaperones. Indicate the number of children and the number of adults.

Amusement Park II 7

1. The entry fee to the Robert's Rides park includes a hot dog and chips. If each student buys a $0.79 drink, approximately how much would your class spend on drinks?

2. Chaperones receive a half-off box lunch. A box lunch costs $3.89. Approximately how much will be spent on lunch for the three chaperones?

8 Amusement Park III

Passengers on the Rocky Roller Coaster at Robert's Rides park sit in six-passenger cars. A car is loaded and released every 30 seconds. Approximately how long would it take for your class and 3 chaperones to be loaded in seconds? in minutes?

9 Divisibility

A number is divisible by:	if the:
2	number ends in 0, 2, 4, 6, or 8
3	sum of the digits is divisible by 3
4	last 2 digits form a number divisible by 4
5	number ends in 0 or 5
6	number is divisible by 2 and 3
9	sum of the digits is divisible by 9

Determine if each number is divisible by the given numbers.

	Number	2	3	4	5	6	9
1.	15,480						
2.	34,650						
3.	75,400						
4.	99,999						
5.	1,000						

Quick Estimate—Decimals 1   10

1. Which is the best estimate for 5.214 + 3.92?
    a. 7.2   b. 9.1   c. 8.0

2. Which is the best estimate for 5.214 − 3.92?
    a. 2.7   b. 2.3   c. 1.3

Estimate or Exact?   11

Explain whether each value is an estimate or an exact value.

1. 3,000 people attended the concert.
2. The ticket cost $24.95.
3. Jamie rides bus number 71.
4. The Earth is 93,000,000 miles from the sun.

Connect Ten   12

A quick way to add several single-digit numbers is to connect the numbers that total ten, count the number of connections, multiply by 10, and add any nonconnected numbers.

Find the sum of:

3   5   2   9   8   1   5   5   9   3   2

4   7   6   4   6   9   2   1   7   8   5

13 Counting by the Hundreds

To estimate the sum of multidigit numbers, connect pairs of numbers that have sums approximately equal to a multiple of 100.

Example: 37 + 160 ≈ 200. Find the sum of your connections and the remaining numbers.

221	68	150	309	160 —200— 37
130	149	180	31	19	92

14 Meaningful Metrics—
Temperature

1. It is 30°C. Should you wear short sleeves or a heavy sweater?

2. Should the temperature in a refrigerator be 5°C or 50°C?

> 0°C—water freezes
> 37°C—normal body temperature
> 100°C—water boils

3. An outdoor bank temperature sign reads 25°. Everyone is wearing a coat. Should the temperature be labeled °C or °F?

15 Quick Estimate—
Whole Numbers II

1. Which is the best estimate for 852 x 42?
   a. 32,000   b. 36,000   c. 40,000

2. Which is the best estimate for 852 ÷ 42?
   a. 2   b. 20   c. 200

Front-End Estimation — 16

1. Estimate the sum by rounding each amount to the nearest $1.00?

2. Estimate the sum by adding the dollars and rounding the cents to the nearest 10¢. (Called "front-end estimation.")

$ 2.67
7.17
8.88
10.81
5.52
3.41

3. Which is a closer estimate? Explain.

Quick Estimate— Decimals II — 17

1. Which is the best estimate for 5.25 × 2.4?
   a. 10   b. 13   c. 15

2. Which is the best estimate for 5.25 ÷ 2.4?
   a. 2   b. 0.2   c. 5

Quick Estimate—Angles I — 18

Estimate the measure of the angle:

25°   45°   65°   85°

19 Shady Rectangles

Estimate the area of each shaded region.
Each square represents 4 square inches.

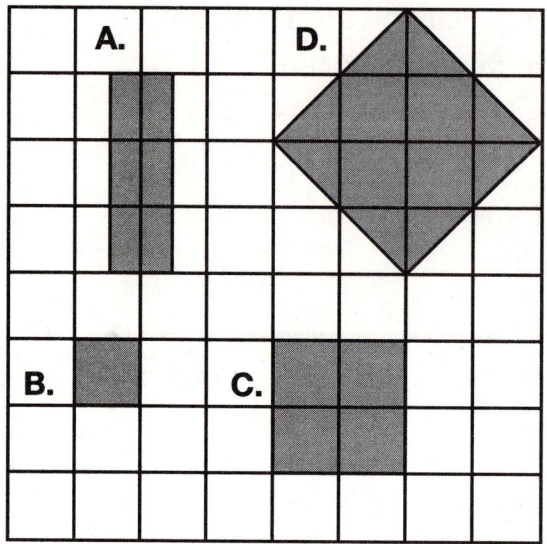

20 First Flight

1. In 1903, Orville Wright piloted the first successful flight a distance of 120 feet. What is a reasonable time for that first flight?

   12 nanoseconds   12 seconds   12 minutes   12 hours

2. In 2004, a regional jet flying from Indianapolis to Cleveland takes approximately (choose one)

   47 nanoseconds   47 seconds   47 minutes   47 hours

   from take-off to landing—a distance of approximately (choose one)

   3,000 feet   30,000 feet   300 miles   3,000 miles

Fraction Benchmarks I — 21

A benchmark is a reference used for comparison. Fraction benchmarks are whole numbers and commonly used fractions. You can compare other fractions to what you know about these benchmarks.

For each number state the closest benchmark: $0, \frac{1}{4}, \frac{1}{2}, \frac{3}{4}, 1$

1. $\frac{9}{10}$
2. $\frac{2}{33}$
3. $\frac{7}{12}$
4. $\frac{7}{9}$
5. $\frac{2}{21}$
6. $\frac{17}{21}$
7. $\frac{10}{19}$
8. $\frac{21}{22}$

An Apple a Day — 22

Katie wants to carry 7 apples in one bag. The weights of the apples range from 12 ounces to 15 ounces. If the bag is designed to hold 5 pounds, should Katie put the 7 apples in the bag? Explain

Quick Estimate — Fractions I — 23

1. Which is the best estimate for $\frac{7}{8} + \frac{3}{4}$?

    a. $\frac{10}{12}$ b. 1 c. $1\frac{1}{2}$

2. Which is the best estimate for $\frac{3}{4} - \frac{1}{5}$?

    a. $\frac{1}{2}$ b. 1 c. 2

24 Jenny's Jogging

Write a description of Jenny's jogging based on the graph.

_____
_____
_____
_____
_____
_____
_____

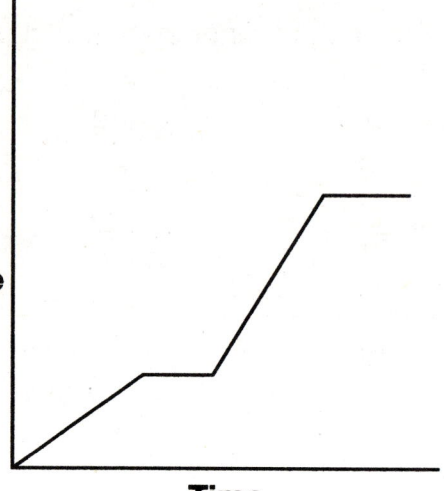

25 Fraction Benchmarks II

Use benchmarks 0, $\frac{1}{2}$, 1, $1\frac{1}{2}$, and 2 to estimate each answer.

1. $\frac{7}{16} + 1\frac{7}{12} + 1\frac{7}{8} \approx$

   _____ + _____ + _____ =

2. $1\frac{4}{5} + \frac{1}{8} + \frac{5}{9} \approx$

   _____ + _____ + _____ =

3. $\frac{2}{5} + 1\frac{8}{9} + \frac{1}{12} \approx$

   _____ + _____ + _____ =

4. $\frac{5}{8} + \frac{9}{10} + 1\frac{3}{5} \approx$

   _____ + _____ + _____ =

The "Round Table" I — 26

Complete the table by rounding each number to the indicated place value.

	Number	Thousands	Hundreds	Tens
1.	3,455			
2.	2,503			
3.	98,765			
4.	123,456			
5.	70,605			

Danny's Decimals — 27

Use estimation to determine which 3 problems Danny missed. Correct them.

1. $23.5 + 0.42 = \underline{27.7}$

2. $5.4 - 0.27 = \underline{5.13}$

3. $0.5 \times 0.8 = \underline{0.4}$

4. $48 \div 0.2 = \underline{240}$

5. $0.5(5.62 - 3.4) = \underline{2.2}$

6. $2.2(6.2 + 0.8) = \underline{1.54}$

28 A "Foot" but Not 12 Inches

Work with a partner.

1. Have your partner count the number of "shoe units" as you walk heel-toe-heel-toe from your desk to a wall. Record the distance. _____

2. Have your partner measure the length of your shoe to the nearest $\frac{1}{2}$ inch.
   1 shoe unit = _____ in.

3. Convert the distance you measured to inches. _____
   Repeat steps 1 – 3 reversing the roles: 1. _____
                                                                                                       2. _____
                                                                                                       3. _____

Why is a shoe unit not a standard unit of measure?

29 On the Bench

For each number write the closest benchmark: 0, $\frac{1}{2}$, 1, $1\frac{1}{2}$, or 2. Then estimate the sums or differences.

1. $1\frac{1}{5} + \frac{7}{8} + 1\frac{8}{9} + \frac{5}{8} + 2\frac{1}{3} + \frac{2}{9} \approx$

   ____ + ____ + ____ + ____ + ____ + ____ = ____

2. $(2\frac{1}{7} + 1\frac{8}{9}) - (\frac{8}{9} + \frac{3}{7}) - (\frac{5}{6} + 1\frac{1}{10}) \approx$

   (____ + ____) − (____ + ____) − (____ + ____) = ____

3. $1\frac{7}{8} - (\frac{4}{5} - \frac{3}{8}) - (\frac{2}{5} - \frac{1}{10}) \approx$

   ____ − (____ − ____) − (____ − ____) = ____

Scavenger Hunt — 2-D Geometry Shapes 30

Describe an object in your classroom that approximates each geometric shape listed.

1. square
2. nonsquare rectangle
3. right triangle
4. equilateral triangle
5. circle
6. concentric (same center) circles

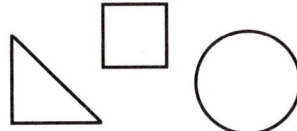

Bag of Apples 31

Brandon paid $2.65 for 2 pounds of apples. At that rate, what is a good estimate for how many pounds of apples he could buy for $10?

It's Been Rounded 32

What range of whole numbers would round to each value?

1. 2,340 to the nearest ten
2. 56,700 to the nearest hundred
3. 14,000 to the nearest thousand
4. 14,000 to the nearest hundred
5. 14,000 to the nearest ten

33 Quick Estimate—Fractions II

1. Which is the best estimate for $7\frac{3}{4} + 5\frac{7}{8}$?
   a. $12\frac{1}{2}$ b. $13\frac{1}{2}$ c. $14\frac{1}{2}$

2. Which is the best estimate for $7\frac{3}{4} - 5\frac{7}{8}$?
   a. 2   b. $2\frac{1}{2}$ c. 3

34 Movie Magic

Mr. Marcus wants to purchase a $1489 camera system for the photography class. The class account has $500. The photography class decides to hold fundraisers the tenth of each month starting October 10. If the class raises $125 each month, will Mr. Marcus have enough money to buy and use the camera at the May 25 awards assembly?

35 The "Round Table" II

Complete the table by rounding each number to the indicated place value.

Number	Tens	Ones	Tenths	Hundreths
1. 34.551				
2. 7.513				
3. 108.765				
4. 2.345				
5. 70.605				

Quick Estimate—Fractions III 36

1. Which is the best estimate for $2\frac{3}{4} \times 4\frac{5}{8}$?

    a. 10   b. $12\frac{1}{2}$ c. 15

2. Which is the best estimate for $2\frac{3}{4} \div 4\frac{5}{8}$?

    a. $\frac{1}{2}$ b. 1   c. 2

Calendar Math 37

JULY						
Sun	Mon	Tue	Wed	Thu	Fri	Sat
	1	2	3	4	5	6
7	8	9	10	11	12	13
14	15	16	17	18	19	20
21	22	23	24	25	26	27
28	29	30	31			

1. Find the sum of the numbers in the shaded region.
2. Explain how you can quickly find the sum of any 3-by-3 region on the calendar without actually adding the numbers.
3. What's the sum of the 3-by-3 region with 12 in the center?

38 Ben's Bedroom

Ben's bedroom is 11'10" by 10'. The carpet he wants is $2.95 per square foot. The pad and installation will cost $79.99. What is a reasonable estimate for the carpet, pad, and installation?

10'

11'10"

39 Fashionable Fabric

Felicia bought $2\frac{7}{8}$ yards of periwinkle blue material and $3\frac{3}{4}$ yards of navy blue fabric to make pillows for her room. To the nearest yard, how much fabric did Felicia buy?

40 Fraction Benchmarks III

For each fraction, write the appropriate benchmark: 0, $\frac{1}{4}$, $\frac{1}{2}$, $\frac{3}{4}$, or 1

1. $\frac{4}{7}$
2. $\frac{73}{99}$
3. $\frac{29}{60}$
4. $\frac{5}{18}$
5. $\frac{9}{98}$
6. $\frac{9}{19}$
7. $\frac{9}{10}$
8. $\frac{9}{35}$

All the Way Home — 41

1. On May 10, Hillary walked home from school. Which distance would be a reasonable distance for her to walk?

   1.5 mm   1.5 cm   1.5 m   1.5 km

2. If Hillary lives in Omaha, which outdoor temperature is reasonable?

   12°C   22°C   12°F   22°F

Flower Garden — 42

Estimate the fractional part for each type of flower.

marigolds	daisies	tulips
daffodils		roses
peonies		

1. daffodils _____   **3.** marigolds _____   **5.** roses _____

2. daisies _____   **4.** peonies _____   **6.** tulips _____

43 Betty's Breakfast

Select the most likely measurement for each item Betty has for breakfast:

1. glass of juice	200 mL	2 L	20 L
2. 2 pieces of toast	50 g	5.0 kg	50 kg
3. cereal	35 mg	35 g	35 kg
4. milk for cereal	1 mL	100mL	1 L

44 Scavenger Hunt—
3-D Geometry Shapes

Describe an object in your classroom that approximates each geometric shape listed.

1. cube _____

2. rectangular prism _____

3. pyramid _____

4. sphere _____

5. cylinder _____

6. cone _____

45 Grocery Shopping

Kelly had the following items in her grocery cart:

lettuce 89¢

3 cans of soup, 99¢ each

flour tortillas $1.29

eggs $1.39

ground turkey $1.49

cheese $1.09

3 cartons of milk, 3 for $5.00

sour cream $1.89

Estimate the cost by rounding each item to the nearest $0.50.

Theater Treats 46

You have $15. Can you buy 3 candy bars ($1.29 each), 3 drinks (99¢ each) and 3 boxes of popcorn ($1.99 each)?

Flying the Flag 47

For each flag, estimate the fraction that is white:

1.
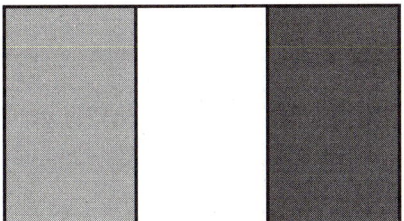

3.
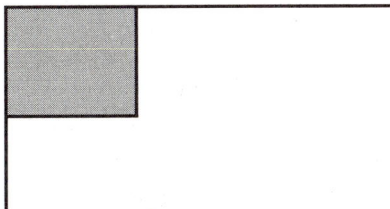

2.
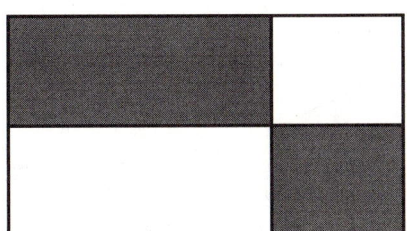

4.
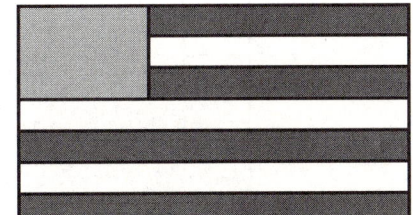

48 Capital Cities

The Shermans traveled from Columbus, Ohio, to Indianapolis, Indiana, a distance of approximately 185 miles.

1. If their car averages 29.7 mpg, estimate the amount of gas used.

2. If gas costs $1.49/gallon, estimate the cost of gasoline for the trip.

49 Shady Areas I

Estimate the area of each shaded region. Each square represents 1 square foot.

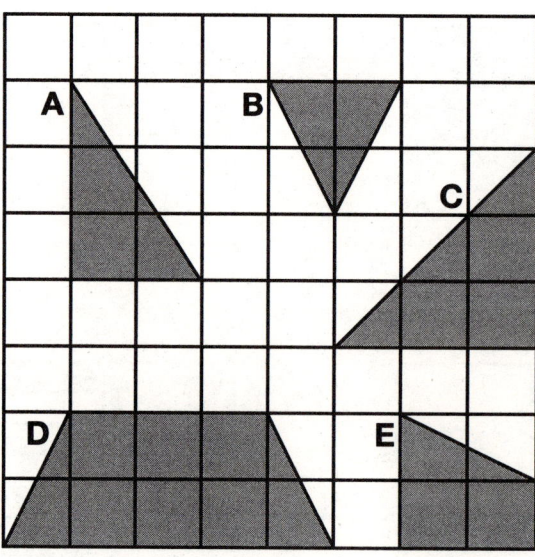

Quick Estimate—Angles II | 50

Estimate the measure of the angle:

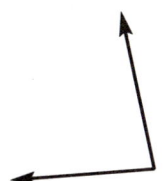   45°   85°   95°   125°

Inchworm, Inchworm | 51

Give the location of each letter.

A _____   D _____
B _____   E _____
C _____

Centipede | 52

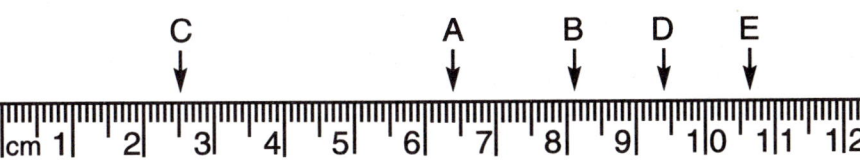

Give the value of each letter to the nearest 0.5 cm.

A _____   D _____
B _____   E _____
C _____

53 I Don't Know, But . . .

When asked the following questions, you might not know the answers. But if you consider the answer choices, you should be able to determine the correct answers. What are the answers?

1. Over a short distance, how fast can a cheetah run?
   A. 60 ft./hr.   B. 6 mi./hr.   C. 60 mi./hr.   D. 600 mi./hr.

2. What is the distance between Dallas and Houston, Texas?
   A. 250 yd.   B. 25 mi.   C. 250 mi.   D. 2,500 mi.

3. How large is a car's gas tank?
   A. 15 qt.   B. 15 gal.   C. 150 qt.   D. 150 gal.

4. How wide is a standard front door?
   A. 1 ft.   2. $1\frac{1}{2}$ ft.   C. 1 yd.   D. $1\frac{1}{2}$ yd.

54 When Does 50 Equal 110?

A quick way to calculate a weight in pounds when the actual weight is given in kilograms is double the weight in kilograms and add a tenth.

Example: for 50 kg, 2 x 50 = 100 and $\frac{1}{10}$ x 100 = 10, so 50 kg ≈ 100 + 10 or 110 lb.

Calculate the weight in pounds.

1. 100 kg ≈ _____ lb.
2. 25 kg ≈ _____ lb.
3. 60 kg ≈ _____ lb.
4. 80 kg ≈ _____ lb.

Party Punch 55

Patty's party punch is made with $\frac{3}{4}$ gal. fruit mix drink and $\frac{3}{4}$ qt. of sherbet. Is there enough punch for a dozen people to each have a 1-cup serving?

Measures

1 cup = 8 oz.
1 pt. = 2 cups
1 qt. = 2 pt.
1 gal. = 4 qt.

Party Time 56

A class of twenty-nine students is planning a surprise birthday party for the teacher. Estimate the cost of party supplies.

Note: The items are sold in packages and cannot be bought individually.

Party Supplies

Plates	10 for $1.99
Napkins	16 for $1.49
Cups	10 for $1.49
Forks	18 for $1.89

Summer Job 57

The graph shows what Joanie can earn working part-time at Ed's Eatery and at Dontae's Deli. For what range of hours will she earn more working at Ed's Eatery? at Dontae's Deli?

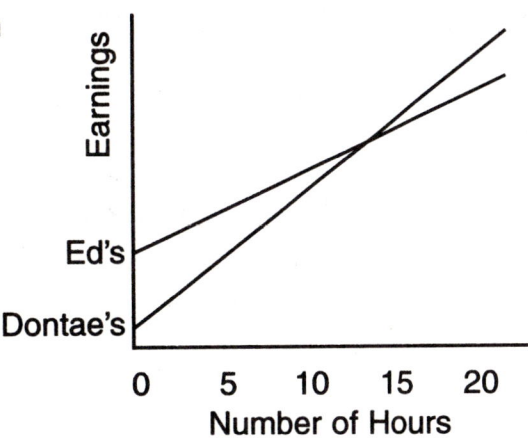

58 Metric Match

Match each item to the best measurement estimate.

_____ 1. carton of milk   a. 60 centimeters
_____ 2. height of flagpole   b. 3.8 liters
_____ 3. weight of an adult   c. 75 kilograms
_____ 4. gasoline purchase   d. 5 meters
_____ 5. length of arm   e. 75 liters

59 Carl's Clothing

Carl has $150. Is that enough to buy two shirts priced for $19.99 each, one pair of jeans for $24.99, two pairs of socks for $2.25 a pair, and shoes for $74.99?

60 Possible Products

Use estimation and number sense to determine the correct product without doing the multiplication.

1. 256 x 135 =   a. 24,560   b. 3,456   c. 34,560
2. 22 x 116 =   a. 2,558   b. 2,552   c. 252
3. 120 x 140 =   a. 26,800   b. 1,680   c. 16,800
4. How did you determine the correct product for number 3?

X Marks the Spot — 61

Mark an X at the location of $\frac{1}{2}$ on each number line.

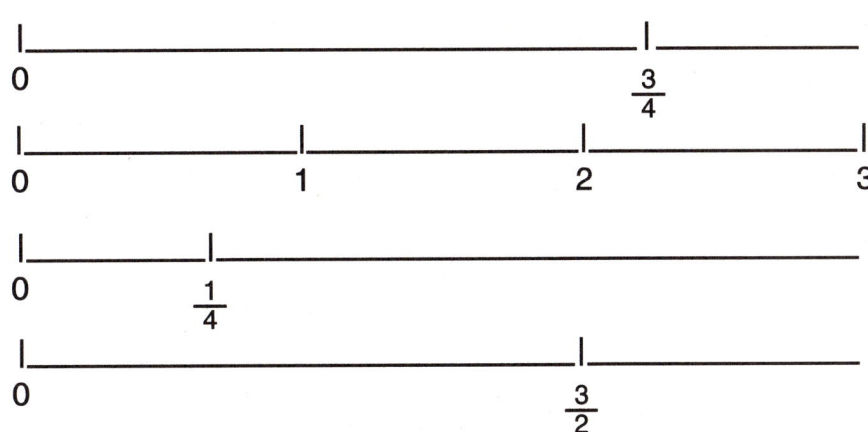

Kayleigh's Account — 62

On Monday, Kayleigh had $327.12 in her checking account. On Tuesday, she wrote a check for $32.17. She then made a deposit of $25.98 on Wednesday and withdrew $15.00 on Thursday. On Friday, does she have more or less than $300 in her account?

Meat Packing — 63

The sliced-meat packages at the deli counter range from 1 lb. 4 oz. to 2 lb. 2 oz. What is a reasonable range for the weight of 10 packages?

10–13 lb.   21–30 lb.

13–21 lb.   more than 30 lb.

64 Polly's Painting

Polly made an abstract painting. Each color is what fractional part of the painting?

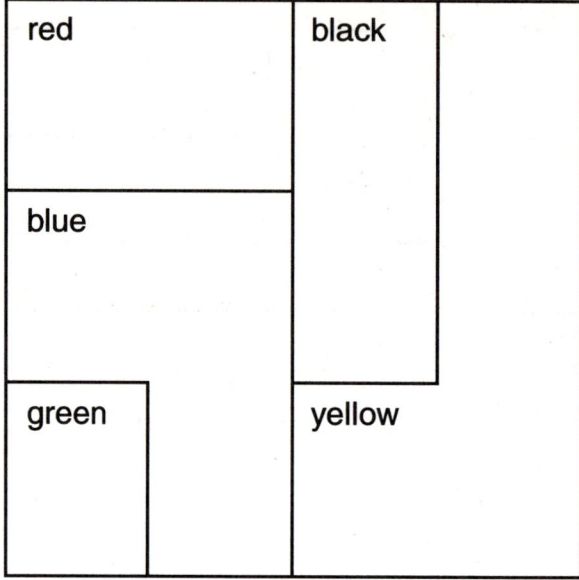

65 Mixed-Up Multiplication

Use estimation to determine which 4 problems Mike missed. Explain his errors.

1. $\frac{2}{5} \times \frac{2}{5} = \frac{4}{5}$

2. $\frac{3}{10} \times \frac{3}{10} = \frac{9}{10}$

3. $\frac{1}{2} \times \frac{1}{2} = \frac{1}{4}$

4. $\frac{3}{4} \times \frac{3}{4} = 2\frac{1}{4}$

5. $\frac{3}{2} \times \frac{3}{2} = 4\frac{1}{2}$

To the Point — 66

Locate each point on the number line.

A $\frac{3}{4} + \frac{1}{2}$ **C** $\frac{3}{4} \times \frac{1}{2}$

B $\frac{3}{4} - \frac{1}{2}$ **D** $\frac{3}{4} \div \frac{1}{2}$

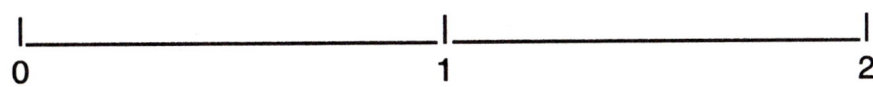

Travelogue — 67

Use the graph to complete the table of Terry's travel from Toledo to Columbus.

Time	Distance
0 hr.	0 mi.
$\frac{1}{2}$ hr.	_____
1 hr.	_____
$1\frac{1}{2}$ hrs.	_____
2 hrs.	_____
$2\frac{1}{2}$ hrs.	_____
3 hrs.	_____
$3\frac{1}{2}$ hrs.	_____

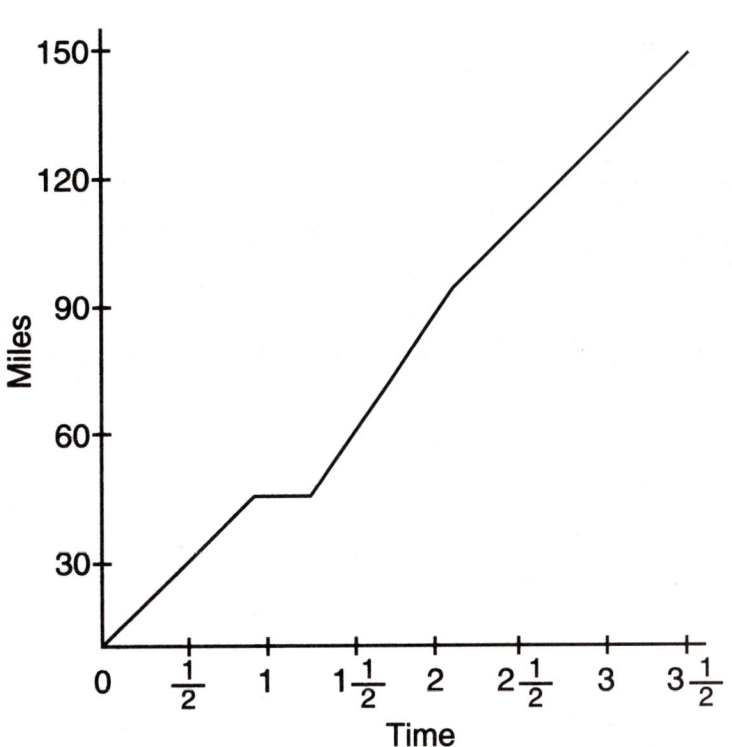

68 Clustering I

The numbers in each set "cluster" around a number that can be used to estimate the sum.

Example: $4.1 + 3.95 + 4.08 + 3.89 + 4.15 \approx 4 + 4 + 4 + 4 + 4$ or 5×4 or 20
Use clustering to estimate each sum.

1. $6.12 + 6.06 + 5.96 + 5.8 \approx$ _____
2. $8.96 + 9.17 + 8.88 + 9.03 + 9.03 \approx$ _____
3. $\$14.76 + \$15.12 + \$14.81 + \$14.90 + \$15.05 + \$15.11 \approx$ _____

69 Advertising

Charlie stuffs advertisements into envelopes. He averages 12 envelopes per minute. At this rate, Charlie can stuff 1,200 envelopes in

a. 1 to 2 hours   b. 3 to 5 hours   c. 10 to 11 hours   d. 12 hours

70 Shady Strips

Shade each strip to show the given percent. Explain how you determined what to shade.

1. 90%   2. 15%   3. 60%

© McGraw-Hill Children's Publishing

Shady Areas II 71

Estimate the area of the shaded region.
Each square represents 4 square inches.

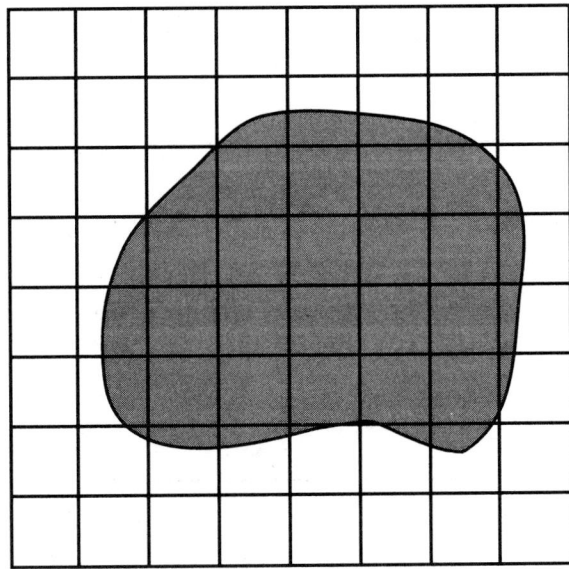

Benchmark Fractions IV 72

Use benchmarks 0, $\frac{1}{2}$, 1, $1\frac{1}{2}$, and 2 to estimate the answers to these subtraction problems.

1. $1\frac{7}{16} - \frac{1}{12} - \frac{5}{9} \approx$

2. $1\frac{4}{5} - \frac{1}{8} - \frac{5}{9} \approx$

3. $2\frac{1}{12} - 1\frac{2}{9} - \frac{5}{12} \approx$

4. $\frac{7}{8} - \frac{1}{10} - \frac{7}{12} \approx$

73 X Marks Another Spot

Mark the location of $1\frac{1}{2}$ with an X on each number line.

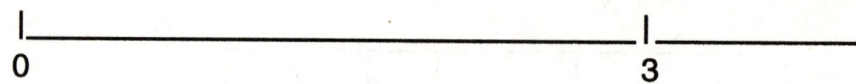

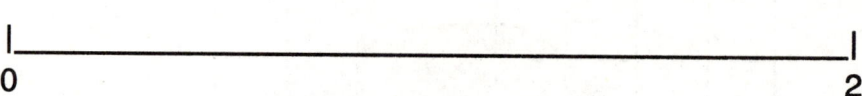

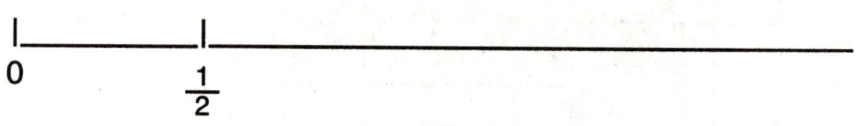

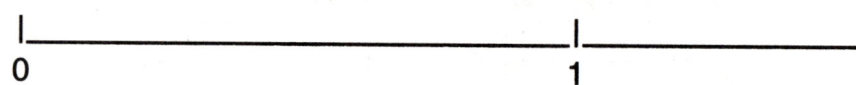

74 Pair Them Up!

Each problem in the first column has the same answer as a problem in the second column. Estimate the solutions to determine the matches.

_____ 1. $7\frac{3}{5} + 2\frac{1}{2}$ a. $6\frac{1}{5} + 2\frac{1}{5}$

_____ 2. $10\frac{3}{5} - 2\frac{1}{5}$ b. $2\frac{3}{4} + 6\frac{1}{3}$

_____ 3. $11\frac{5}{6} - 3\frac{3}{4}$ c. $5\frac{1}{5} + 4\frac{9}{10}$

_____ 4. $4\frac{7}{12} + 4\frac{1}{2}$ d. $3\frac{5}{6} + 4\frac{1}{4}$

Compared to 500 — 75

State whether each quantity is greater than or less than 500.

1. number of students in your school _____
2. number of seconds in an hour _____
3. number of nickles in $20.00 _____
4. number of pages in your math book _____
5. number of feet in a mile _____

How Many Digits? — 76

How many digits are in each answer? Use number sense—you don't have to calculate the answers.

1. 5,296 + 2,310
2. 5,296 + 8,765
3. 5,296 − 96
4. 5,296 − 5,000
5. 52 x 96
6. 52 x 765
7. 6,250 ÷ 25
8. 1,250 ÷ 125

Exercise Estimates — 77

Every morning at 7:30, Marissa follows the same exercise routine: she stretches 5 minutes, runs two 12-minute miles on a treadmill, lifts light weights for $10\frac{1}{2}$ minutes, uses a stepper for 5 minutes 30 seconds, and takes 5.5 minutes to cool down. Approximately what time is it when Marissa completes her exercise routine?

78 Money for Time

Alexis earns $11.80 an hour. Approximately how much will she earn if she works 30 hours? She earns double time for working on a holiday. How much will she earn working 6 hours on the Fourth of July?

79 Clustering II

The addends in each problem are "clustered" around a multiple of ten. To estimate each sum, find the product of that multiple of ten and the number of addends.

1. $27 + 32 + 28 + 29 + 33 + 28 + 31 + 27 \approx$ _____
2. $57 + 62 + 61 + 63 + 59 + 58 \approx$ _____
3. $77 + 83 + 83 + 79 + 81 + 78 + 78 \approx$ _____
4. $47 + 52 + 51 + 53 + 49 + 48 + 50 + 46 + 53 \approx$ _____

80 Which Is Larger?

Which number is larger?

1. $\frac{2}{5}$ or $\frac{2}{3}$
2. $\frac{7}{8}$ or $\frac{8}{9}$
3. $\frac{6}{11}$ or $\frac{7}{15}$
4. $\frac{4}{5}$ or 0.75
5. 0.02 or 0.022

Geometry Scavenger Hunt 81

Describe an object in your classroom that approximates each geometric shape listed.

1. parallel lines
2. right angle
3. perpendicular lines
4. acute angle
5. flip (reflection)
6. turn (rotation)

reflection

Chances Are . . . 82

Estimate the chance (probability) from 0 (never) to 1 (always) that each event will happen. Place the letter of the event above its probability on the number line.

A Tomorrow the sun will rise in the east.
B A toss of a coin will result in a head.
C You will draw a heart from a standard deck of cards.
D You will roll a 2 or 3 on the next roll of a fair die.
E It will be at least 150° F outside tomorrow.

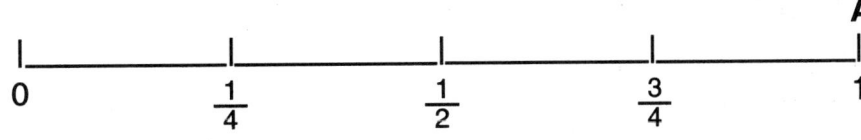

83 Roberto's Reading

Roberto is reading a book that is 425 pages long. He reads between 16 and 20 pages a day. At this rate how long will it take him to read the book?

a. 1–2 weeks
b. 3–4 weeks
c. 21–22 weeks
d. more than 21 weeks

84 Hallway Carpet

A hallway runner measures 4.5' by 21.5'. Which is the best estimate of the area of the runner?

a. 26 sq. ft.
b. 84 sq. ft.
c. 100 sq. ft.
d. 120 sq. ft.

85 Going Around

Compare the circumference of an 8-inch-diameter circle to the perimeter of an 8-inch-sided square. Complete: The circumference is approximately _____ (fractional part) of the perimeter.

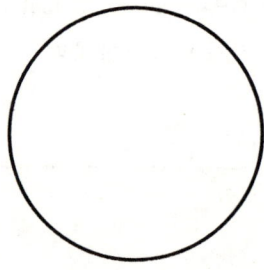

$C = \pi d; \pi \approx 3.14$

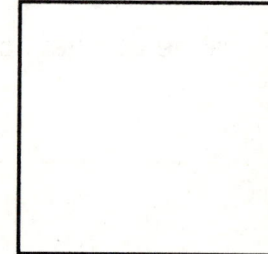

$P = 4s$

Fruit Basket 86

Four pieces of fruit weigh 11 oz., 15 oz., 19 oz., and 10 oz. Which is the best etimate for the total weight of the fruit?

a. 1.5 lb.
b. 2.5 lb.
c. 3.5 lb.
d. 4.5 lb.

Calorie Count 87

A serving of ham and cheesy hash browns contains 15 g fat, 30 g carbohydrates, and 9 g protein. Compare the number of fat calories to the number of calories in a serving.

Calories per gram	
Protein	4
Carbohydrates	4
Fat	9

Grocery Cart 88

1. Estimate the cost of the items in the grocery cart by rounding each to the nearest $1.00.

2. Estimate the cost of the items in the grocery cart by adding the dollars and rounding the cents to the nearest 10¢.

Grocery Cart	
Ground beef	$3.29
Potatoes	$2.99
Lettuce	$0.99
Carrots	$0.79
Dressing	$1.39
Cake	$11.99

89 What's the Temperature?

The formula for converting Celsius to Fahrenheit is $F = \frac{9}{5}C + 32$. To quickly estimate the Fahrenheit temperature when the Celsius temperature is given, double the Celsius temperature and add 30.

Example: $20°C \approx 2 \times 20 + 30 \approx 70°F$

Estimate the Fahrenheit temperature for
    15°C _____   30°C _____   35°C _____

90 To the Point–Decimal Point

Locate each point on the number line.

A $1.5 + 0.25$ **B** $1.1 - 0.2$ **C** 0.5×0.8 **D** $2.8 \div 2.0$

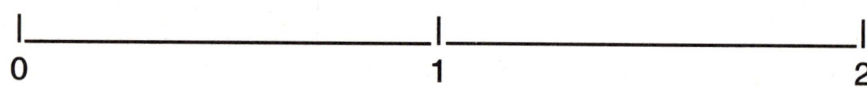

```
|_____|_____|
0                1                2
```

91 Crossing Tennessee

On a map of Tennessee the distance from Memphis to Knoxville measures $4\frac{3}{4}$ inches. If the scale of the map is $\frac{1}{2}$ in. = 40 mi., estimate the distance from Memphis to Knoxville.

Fraction Mismatch 92

Each set of numbers contains three equivalent fractions. Which fraction doesn't belong?

set a	$\frac{30}{45}$	$\frac{14}{21}$	$\frac{9}{10}$	$\frac{18}{27}$
set b	$\frac{50}{60}$	$\frac{15}{35}$	$\frac{10}{12}$	$\frac{30}{36}$
set c	$\frac{2}{3}$	$\frac{4}{9}$	$\frac{16}{36}$	$\frac{8}{18}$
set d	$\frac{24}{64}$	$\frac{12}{32}$	$\frac{3}{8}$	$\frac{2}{4}$

Meaningful Metrics—Volume 93

A milliliter (mL) equals 1 cubic centimeter (cu cm or cm^3).
A liter (L) is a little more than a quart (qt.).

Which is greater?
1. 2 L or 2 qt.
2. 4 mL or a cube measuring 2 cm on one edge
3. a 50-L gas tank or a 15-gal. gas tank
4. Would a drinking glass hold 300 mL or 3 L?
5. Would a fish tank hold 80 mL or 80 L of water?

Smart Shopping 94

Which is a better deal?

Barb's Bike Shop

All $89.99 Bikes
Extra $\frac{1}{10}$ Off!

Cecil's Cycles

All $89.99 Bikes
$10 Mail-In Rebate

95 Esti - metrics

Determine the best estimate for each measurement.

Measurements Facts

1 cm—less than $\frac{1}{2}$ inch (10 mm)
1 m—longer than 1 yd. (100 cm)
1 km—0.6 mile (1000 m)

1. length of yardstick   91 mm   91 cm   91 m
2. width of notebook paper   21.5 mm   2.15 cm   21.5 cm
3. length of paper clip   3 mm   30 mm   30 cm
4. length of football field   120 m   12 km   120 km
5. thickness of paper clip wire 1 mm   1 cm   1 m

96 Benchmark Fractions V

Use benchmarks 0, $\frac{1}{2}$, 1, $1\frac{1}{2}$, and 2 to estimate each answer.

1. $\frac{7}{16} + 1\frac{1}{12} + 1\frac{4}{9} \approx$
   ____ + ____ + ____ =

2. $1\frac{4}{5} - \frac{1}{8} - \frac{5}{9} \approx$
   ____ - ____ - ____ =

3. $\frac{7}{12} \times 1\frac{8}{9} \approx$
   ____ × ____ =

4. $\frac{7}{8} \div 1\frac{9}{10} \approx$
   ____ ÷ ____ =

Tips for Tipping I — 97

One way to calculate a 15% tip is to compute 10% (move the decimal point 1 place to the left) and then add $\frac{1}{2}$ of that amount.

Example: To find 15% of $48.00, 10% ($48.00) = $4.80; $4.80 + $2.40 = $7.20 tip

Estimate a 15% tip for

1. $30.00   **2.** $44.00   **3.** $90.00

Tips for Tipping II — 98

One way to calculate a 20% tip is to compute 10% (move decimal point 1 place to the left) and double that amount.

Example: 20% of $48.00 = 10%($48.00) x 2 = $4.80 x 2 = $9.60

Calculate a 20% tip for

1. $91.00   **2.** $55.00   **3.** $125.00   **4.** $24.00

Being Close Counts — 99

1. Which fraction is closest to 1? $\frac{4}{5}$ $\frac{44}{45}$ $\frac{11}{15}$

2. Which decimal is closest to 1?   0.91   0.9   0.099

3. Which number is closest to 1? $\frac{2}{3}$ 0.66   0.67

100 A Piece of the Pie

Estimate the number of degrees in each sector of the pie graph.

apple _____

cherry _____

peach _____

blueberry _____

pecan _____

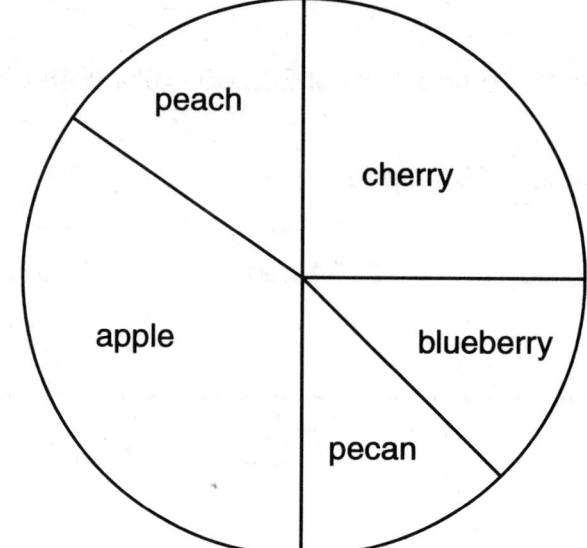

101 Round Up, Round Down

The usual rule for rounding is: If the digit to the right of the indicated place value is 5 or greater, round up. Otherwise, round down.

Example: Round to the nearest integer: $2.7 \approx 3$; $2.4 \approx 2$; $2.5 \approx 3$

Some situations require other rules for rounding. Work with a partner. Discuss whether each result should be rounded up or down. Explain.

1. buying paint for a room that measures 11.9' by 14.4' by 8'
2. a box can hold 8.7 cans
3. the weight computation for a ride allows for 24.6 passengers

Compatible Numbers   102

Compatible numbers are reasonable estimates in numbers that are easily computed.

Example $37\frac{1}{4} \div 5\frac{7}{8} \approx 36 \div 6 = 6$

Use compatible numbers to estimate each quotient.

1. $29\frac{1}{3} \div 7\frac{1}{8} \approx$

2. $51\frac{1}{4} \div 5\frac{1}{16} \approx$

3. $47\frac{1}{4} \div 6\frac{1}{16} \approx$

4. $34\frac{3}{4} \div 7\frac{1}{16} \approx$

The Survey Says . . .   103

In a survey, 4 out of 5 people said they watched the evening news.

1. Which is a reasonable number of viewers in a town of 12,420 residents?
   a. 1,000   b. 6,000   c. 10,000

2. Which is a reasonable number of viewers in a city of 161,095 residents?
   a. 13,000   b. 130,000   c. 150,00

104 Morning Walk

The graph shows Toni's distance from her house during her morning walk from 7:00 A.M. to 8:00 A.M. Write a story about Toni's walk.

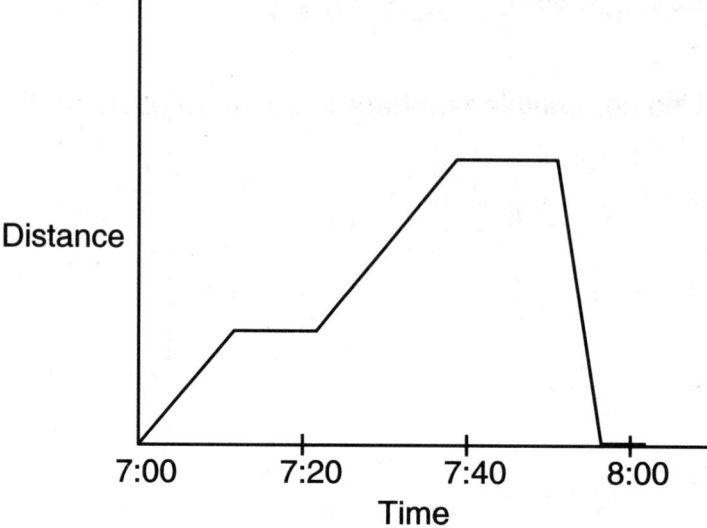

105 Possible Percents

A *benchmark* is a reference used for comparison. Percent benchmarks represent whole numbers and commonly used fractions. You can compare other percents to what you know about these benchmarks. Use benchmark percents to determine the correct answers without performing the multiplications.

Benchmarks: 1% is $\frac{1}{100}$ of the original.
50% is half of the original.
100% is the original.
Greater than 100% is more than the original.

1. 40% of 2,250 is   a. 900   b. 1,125   c. 9,000
2. 140% of 26,320 is   a. 3,848   b. 36,848   c. 52,640
3. 90% of 5,250 is   a. 47.25   b. 472.5   c. 4725
4. 0.2% of 96,120 is   a. 192.24   b. 1922.4   c. 19,224

Running 106

The graph shows the distance Morgan runs everyday. Write what might have happened—

1. from 3:30 to 3:45
2. from 3:45 to 4:00
3. from 4:00 to 4:15
4. from 4:15 to 4:30

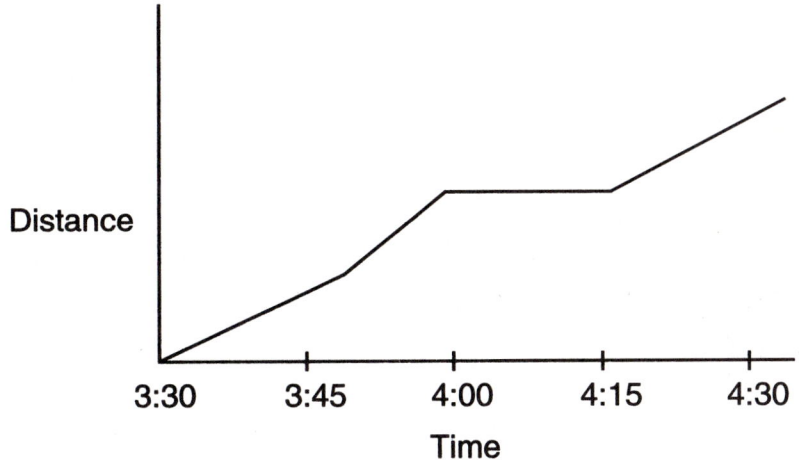

Percent Areas 107

Plot the points. Connect them in order. Then, estimate the percent of the grid in the figure formed. (Remember that the first number in a coordinate pair is the horizontal distance from zero and the second number is the vertical distance from zero.)

(4,6), (4,7), (5,8), (3,8), (1,7), (3,7), (3,6), (2.5,5), (2,4), (3,3), (6,3), (7,5), (7,6), (8,8), (6,8), (6,6), (4,6)

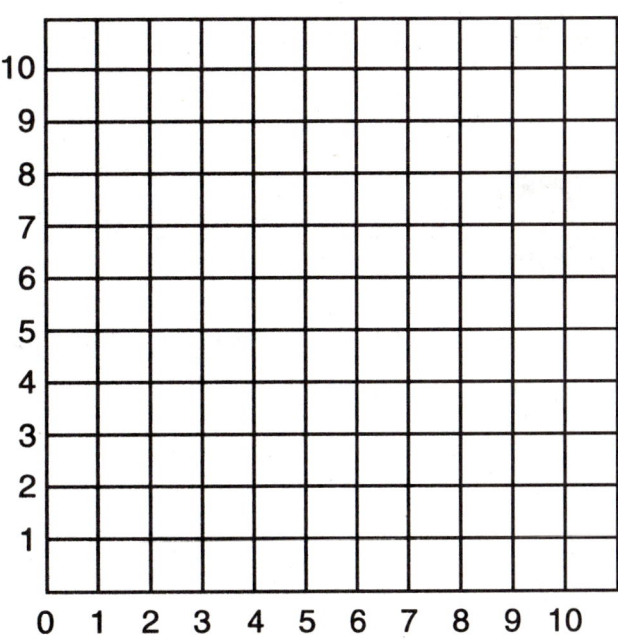

108 Crafty Carpentry

For a craft project, Carol must have strips of wood in lengths of 8 in., $\frac{1}{2}$ yd., $1\frac{1}{2}$ ft., and $\frac{3}{4}$ yd. Can Carol cut all the strips from a piece of wood 6 ft. long? Explain.

109 The Answer Is . . .

Read each problem carefully and answer the question.

1. You have 50 tokens to distribute fairly to 12 children. How many tokens will each child receive?
2. A ferry can carry 12 cars at a time. How many trips will it take to transport 50 cars?
3. How many eggs will be left over when 50 eggs are placed in dozen cartons? Compare the answers.

110 Travel Notes

1. The Ramirez's took a trip by car. Mrs. Ramirez drove for five hours with one 15-minute stop. What is a reasonable distance for the trip?
2. Averaging 50 mph, approximately how long will it take to drive 302 miles?

Prediction | 111

Make a scatter plot of the data.

Time (hrs.)	Medicine (mg)
0	1000
2	750
4	562
6	421
8	316
10	237
12	178

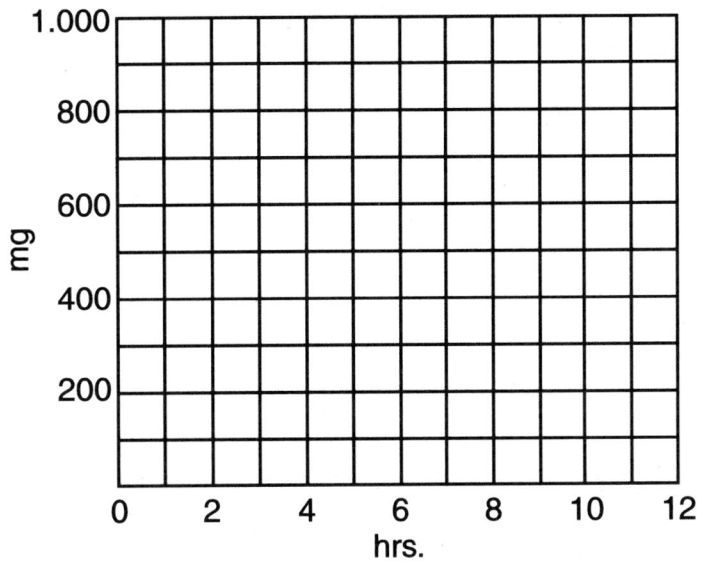

Estimate the amount of medicine that remains after

3 hrs. _____   7 hrs. _____   11 hrs. _____

Fractured Fractions | 112

One way to estimate a product of two fractions is to use a rounded whole number for one fraction, split the other fraction into parts, and multiply the whole number by each part.

Example: $5\frac{5}{6} \times 3\frac{2}{3} \approx 6 \times 3\frac{2}{3}$; $(6 \times 3) + (6 \times \frac{2}{3}) = 18 + 4 = 22$

Estimate the products:

1. $7\frac{9}{10} \times 5\frac{1}{4} \approx$

2. $9\frac{1}{11} \times 6\frac{1}{3} \approx$

3. $11\frac{6}{7} \times 3\frac{5}{6} \approx$

113 Casey's Confusion

Use estimation and number sense to find and correct the three errors Casey made.

1. $1\frac{1}{2} + 1\frac{1}{3} = 2\frac{5}{6}$

2. $\frac{5}{7} + \frac{5}{7} = \frac{10}{14}$

3. $1\frac{7}{8} - 1\frac{1}{2} = \frac{3}{8}$

4. $\frac{3}{5} - \frac{1}{2} = \frac{2}{3}$

5. $4\frac{2}{3} + 4\frac{3}{4} = 8\frac{5}{12}$

6. $6\frac{1}{4} - 2\frac{3}{4} = 3\frac{1}{2}$

114 Two Out of Three . . .

Two out three dentists recommend Super-Smile Toothpaste.

1. Which is the best estimate for the number recommending the toothpaste at a conference of 24,132 dentists?
   a. 12,000   b. 16,000   c. 20,000

2. Which is the best estimate for the number not recommending the toothpaste in a city with of 62 dentists?
   a. 41   b. 31   c. 21

115 Border and Carpet

Estimate the amount of wallpaper border (ft.) and carpet (sq. ft.) needed for a room that measures 12'1" by 9'10".

12'1"

9'10"

Percent Choices 116

Choose the best estimate for each problem. Do not compute exact answers.

Benchmarks
$25\% = \frac{1}{4}$ $50\% = \frac{1}{2}$ $75\% = \frac{3}{4}$ $100\% = 1$

1. 22% of 60 is about   a. 12   b. 22   c. 30

2. 95% of 160 is about   a. 15   b. 150   c. 159

3. 70% of 42 is about   a. 11   b. 28   c. 40

4. 1% of 390 is about   a. 4   b. 40   c. 390

5. 150% of 82 is about   a. 40   b. 95   c. 120

How Much? 117

The table gives the data of the number of people willing to pay certain prices for a pound of mixed candy.

1. Plot the data.

Price/lb.	Buyers
$1.50	44
$1.75	33
$2.00	24
$2.25	15
$2.50	6

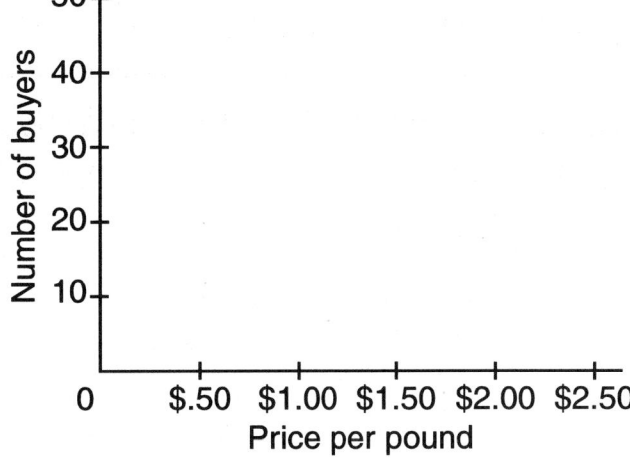

2. From your graph, estimate the number of people who would pay

   $1.60 _____ $2.10 _____ $2.45 _____

118 Percent Benchmarks 1

Choose the best percent estimate for each statement.

Benchmarks						
0%	10%	25%	50%	75%	90%	100%

1. _____ of the students in my class are boys.
2. _____ of the students in my class are left-handed.
3. _____ of the students in my class are wearing athletic shoes.
4. _____ of the school buses are yellow.
5. _____ of the students are more than 7 feet tall.

Complete:

6. 0% of _____.
7. 100% of _____.

119 Chicken Soup Calories

1. A serving of chicken noodle soup contains 2 g fat, 8 g carbohydrates, and 3 g protein. Estimate the number of calories. _____

Calories per gram	
Protein	4
Carbohydrates	4
Fat	9

2. If sleeping burns 30 calories per half hour, a nap of approximately _____ hour(s) would equal a serving of soup.

Penny for Your Thoughts — 120

1. If you stack 1,000 pennies on top of each other, which measure is reasonable for the height of the stack?

    a. 9.5 in.   b. 9.5 ft.   c. 95 ft.   d. 950 ft.

2. If you place 1,000 pennies in a line next to each other, which measure is reasonable for the length of the line of pennies?

    a. 6.2 in.   b. 6.2 ft.   c. 62 ft.   d. 620 ft.

Circle Graphs — 121

Estimate the fraction of each region.

1.
A _____
B _____
C _____
D _____

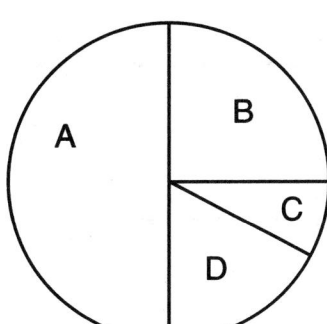

2.
A _____
B _____
C _____
D _____

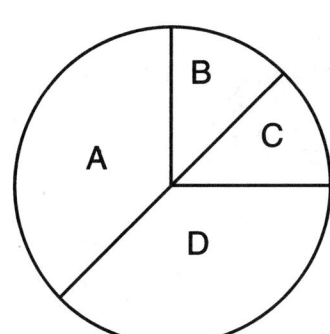

122 Floor Tiles

Jean and Frank decide to tile the hallway in their home. The hall measures 6' by 12'.

1. How many 12"-x-12" tiles do they need?
2. How many 9"-x-9" tiles do they need?
(Hint: How many 9" are there in 6'? in 12'?)

123 Hailing a Taxi

Ryan takes a taxi to a dental appointment. The driver charges $2.50 plus $1.25 per mile. If the dental office is 8.1 miles away, which is a reasonable charge?

a. $4.00   b. $8.00   c. $12.50   d. $21.50

124 Work Day

Catherine listed how much time she estimates she needs to complete various activities at work. If she stays on schedule, will she be able to do everything between 8 A.M. and 4:30 P.M.?

My Day	
Staff meeting	1.5 hrs.
Voice/e-mail	45 mins.
Business report	60 mins.
Lunch	3/4 hr.
Presentation prep	1 hr. 45 mins.
Travel off-site	1/2 hr.
Marketing pres.	90 mins.
Travel	1/2 hr.
Conference call	1 hr.

School Supplies 125

Isaac bought 3 notebooks ($2.89 each), 3 packs of notebook paper ($.99 each), 10 pencils (10/99¢), and 2 pens ($1.29 each). Which is the best estimate for the cost of the items?

    a. $12.00   b. $15.50   c. $18.50   d. $25.00

Temperature Timetable 126

Temperature (°F) of hot water poured into two cans

Time (mins.)	0	10	20	30	40	50	60
Can 1	210°	118°	86°	76°	70°	68°	68°
Can 2	210°	166°	130°	100°	82°	72°	68°

Estimate the temperature of the water in each can at

1. 5 mins. _____ _____
2. 15 mins. _____ _____
3. 25 mins. _____ _____
4. 35 mins. _____ _____
5. 45 mins. _____ _____
6. 55 mins. _____ _____

Going to the Dogs 127

Doug's dog eats eight pounds of Doggie-Delight dog food every seven days. To the nearest hundred pounds, how much Doggie-Delight dog food does Doug's dog eat in a year?

128 Interior-Design Measures

Grace is planning to redo her bedroom. She has to make several measurements. Indicate which unit of measure she will use for each item. (Units may be used more than once.)

Units of Measure
in.
ft.
yd.
sq. ft.
sq. yd.
qt.
gal.

1. height of wall
2. width of door
3. amount of paint for trim
4. amount of carpeting
5. amount of paint for walls
6. drapery rod lengths
7. wallpaper border
8. dimensions of picture frames

129 Project Parts

To complete a project, Pablo needs 11"-long strips of paper that measure $2\frac{1}{2}$", $1\frac{1}{4}$", $1\frac{3}{4}$", and $3\frac{1}{4}$" in width. Will one sheet of $8\frac{1}{2}$"-by-11" paper be enough?

130 Circle Facts

1. What are reasonable estimates for the circumference and the area of the circle?

2. Which two of the following formulas helped you answer question 1?
   a. $P = 4s$
   b. $C = \pi d$
   c. $A = \frac{1}{2}bh$
   d. $F = \frac{9}{5}C + 32$
   e. $A = bh$
   f. $A = \pi r^2$

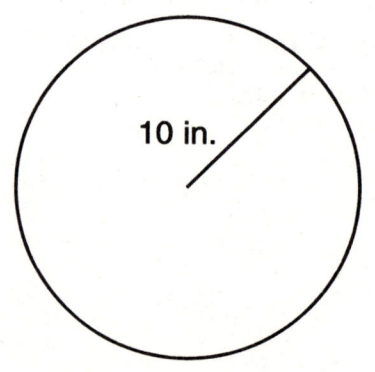
10 in.

Classroom Shapes   131

1. Estimate the length and the width of a rectangular item in your classroom that is not square. Use your estimates to compute the area.

    item: _____   area: _____

2. Estimate the length of a side of a square item in your classroom. Use your estimate to compute the area.

    item: _____   area: _____

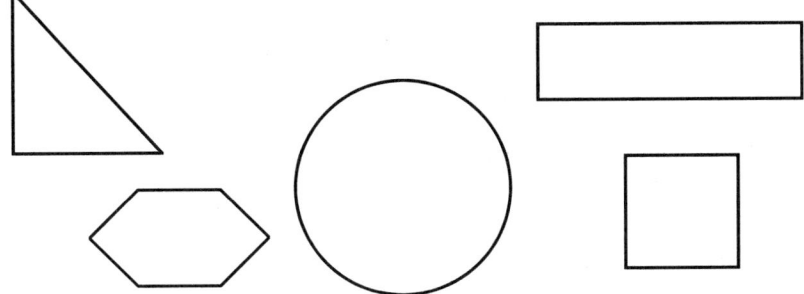

Smart Shoppers   132

Use estimation and number sense to determine if each shopper is a smart shopper. Explain.

1. At Furniture Clearance, a bookcase marked $189 has a $20 instant rebate. Next door, at Bookcase Buyout, the same bookcase is marked $189 but is on sale for an additional $\frac{1}{10}$ off. Taylor decides to buy the bookcase at Furniture Clearance to save money.

2. Jordan argued that an item on sale for $\frac{1}{2}$ off plus an additional $\frac{1}{4}$ off is a better deal than $\frac{1}{4}$ off plus an additional $\frac{1}{2}$ off since the larger fractional part would be subtracted first. (Hint: What would be the two final sale prices for an $80 item?)

133 Is It Cold or Hot?

Choose the most appropriate temperature.

1. preheated oven for baking   350°C   350°F
2. warm summer day in New York City   25°C   25°F
3. inside of a refrigerator   40°C   40°F
4. snowy day in Indianapolis   20°C   20°F

134 Acme Rent-a-Wreck

Acme Rent-a-Wreck charges $25/day and 25¢/mile. What is a reasonable charge for renting a car for two days and driving 395 miles?

a. $75   b. $100   c. $125   d. $150

135 Equation Estimates I

Rewrite each problem using compatible numbers to estimate the solutions.

Example: $49 = 8y$; $48 \approx 8y$ so $y \approx 6$

1. $39 = 19d$; $d \approx$ _____
2. $\frac{26}{w} = 5$; $w \approx$ _____
3. $63 = 31x$; $x \approx$ _____

Handful of Inches — 136

Work with a partner.

1. Measure the span of your hand: _____ in.
2. Measure the following. Use your span and convert to inches.

   desk top: length _____   spans ≈ _____ in.
                width _____   spans ≈ _____ in.

   math book: length _____   spans ≈ _____ in.
                width _____   spans ≈ _____ in.

3. Have your partner do steps 1 and 2.
   Measure partner's span: _____ in.

   Desk top: length _____   spans ≈ _____ in.
                width _____   spans ≈ _____ in.

   Math book: length _____   spans ≈ _____ in.
                width _____   spans ≈ _____ in.

4. Compare your results with your partner's results.

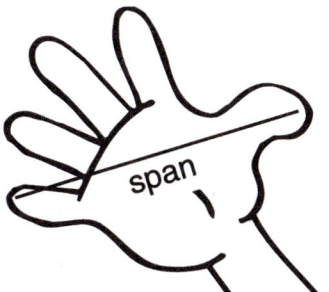

Cricket Temperature — 137

The number of chirps per minute that some crickets make is related to the temperature.

$$t = \frac{ch}{4} + 37,$$

where t is the temperature in °F and ch is the number of chirps per minute. Thus, to get the temperature, divide the chirps/minute by 4 and add 37.

1. One evening, Amy counted 73 chirps in 1 minute. Estimate the temperature.
2. On another evening, she counted 40 chirps in 20 seconds. Estimate the temperature.

138 Celsius Crickets

To estimate the Celsius temperature based on chirping crickets, divide the chirps/minute by 8 and add 5

$$t = \frac{ch}{8} + 5$$

where t is the temperature in °C and ch is the number of chirps per minute.

1. If Pete counted 81 cricket chirps in 1 minute, estimate the temperature in °C.
2. On another evening, Pete counted 40 chirps in 20 seconds. Estimate the temperature in °C.

139 Dartboards

Dakota can choose from two dartboards. Each dartboard measures 24" by 24". Estimate the chance (fraction) of a dart landing on the shaded region of each game board. Which dartboard should Dakota choose for a greater chance to hit the shaded region?

1.
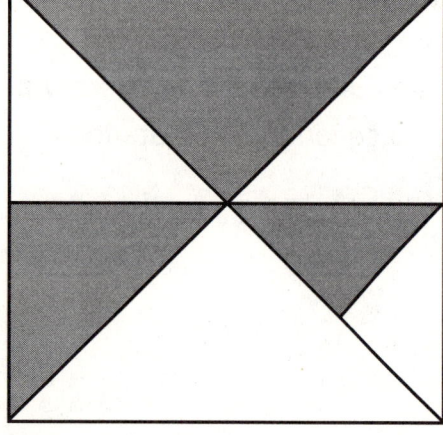

2.
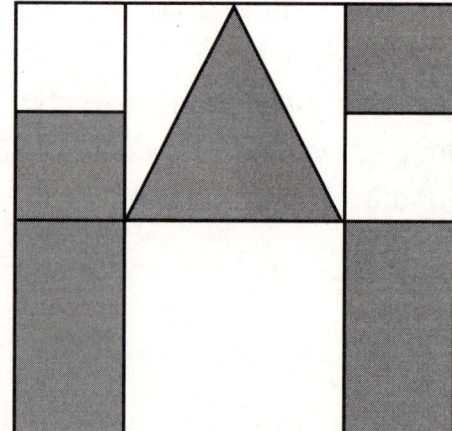

Tally Time 140

Make as many tally marks as you can in 30 seconds. How many did you make? At this rate, how long would it take for you to make

100 marks? _____   1,000 marks? _____   1,000,000 marks? _____

Delivery 141

The weights of 4 packages range from $2\frac{7}{8}$ to $4\frac{7}{8}$ pounds. What is a reasonable estimate for the total weight of the 4 packages?

a. 8–13 lb.
b. 13–18 lb.
c. 18–23 lb.
d. 23–28 lb.

Boston to Washington 142

Boston is approximately 475 miles from Washington, D.C.

1. If the scale on the map is 1 in. = 100 mi., estimate the distance on the map.
2. If Bobby averages 50 mph, how long will it take him to drive from Boston to Washington?

143 Flooring Measurements

A rectangular room measures 11'10" by 17'10".

1. Which is a reasonable estimate for the length of the baseboards?
   a. 30'   b. 50'   c. 60'   d. 216'

2. Which is a reasonable estimate of the area of the room?
   a. 30 sq. ft.   b. 60 sq. ft.   c. 185 sq. ft.   d. 216 sq. ft.

144 Student Solar System

Students were modeling the solar system. One student was the sun. Other students stood a number of steps from the sun to represent the planets. Approximately how far are the first six planets from the sun based on the students' distances?

Planet	Steps from sun	Estimated miles
Mercury	1	31,000,000
Venus	2	
Earth	3	
Mars	$4\frac{1}{2}$	
Jupiter	15	
Saturn	$27\frac{1}{2}$	

Lunar Weights 145

The gravitational pull on the moon is approximately $\frac{1}{6}$ that of the Earth. Thus, a 180-lb. earthling would weigh approximately 30 lb. on the moon. Estimate the following weights.

1. 121-lb. earthling—lunar weight? _____
2. 71-lb. earthling—lunar weight? _____
3. 42-lb. moonling—Earth weight? _____
4. 25-lb. moonling—Earth weight? _____
5. A 156-lb. earthling lost 6 lb. How many lunar pounds did the earthling lose?

Peterson's Print Shop 146

Peterson's Print Shop charges $100 setup fee and 25¢ for each card printed.

1. What is the cost of printing 100 cards?
2. If you can sell the cards for $1.95 each, estimate your profit.

Equation Estimates II 147

Rewrite each problem using rounded numbers to estimate the solutions.

Example: $y + 4\frac{1}{3} = 9\frac{1}{8}$; since $y + 4 \approx 9$, $y \approx 5$

1. $x + 3\frac{1}{6} = 5\frac{9}{10}$; $x \approx$ _____

2. $w - 6\frac{3}{4} = 1\frac{1}{4}$; $w \approx$ _____

3. $y - 2\frac{1}{8} = 3\frac{6}{7}$; $y \approx$ _____

148 What's the Question?

Joaquin left at about 1 P.M. with a full tank of gas. After driving 168 miles, he stopped at 4 P.M. and bought $10.00 worth of gasoline, which filled the tank. The gas cost $1.52/gallon.

1. If the answer is about 55 mph, what is the question?
2. If the answer is about 6.5 gal., what is the question?
3. If the answer is about 25 mpg, what is the question?

149 Compound Areas

For a rectangle: the area equals the base times the height or
$$A = bh$$
For a triangle: the area equals $\frac{1}{2}$ times the base times the height or
$$A = \frac{1}{2}bh$$

Estimate the area of each shape.

1.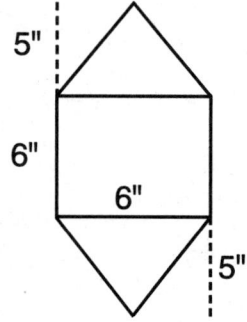

2.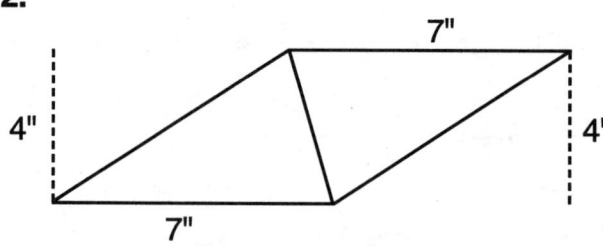

STANDARD N, A

STANDARD G, M

Fraction Tic-Tac-Toe 150

Use estimation and number sense to determine which row, column, or diagonal has a sum of 1.

1.

$\frac{3}{4}$	$\frac{2}{3}$	$\frac{1}{3}$
$\frac{1}{2}$	$\frac{2}{5}$	$\frac{1}{10}$
$\frac{1}{4}$	$\frac{1}{2}$	$\frac{1}{2}$

2.

$\frac{1}{3}$	$\frac{1}{2}$	$\frac{1}{3}$
$\frac{7}{12}$	$\frac{1}{6}$	$\frac{2}{3}$
$\frac{1}{2}$	$\frac{7}{12}$	$\frac{1}{6}$

Fill It Up 151

Estimate the volume of each box to determine which holds the most. Your answer will be in cu. in.

Volume
$V = l \times w \times h$

1. 2.1 in., 5.9 in., 4.2 in.
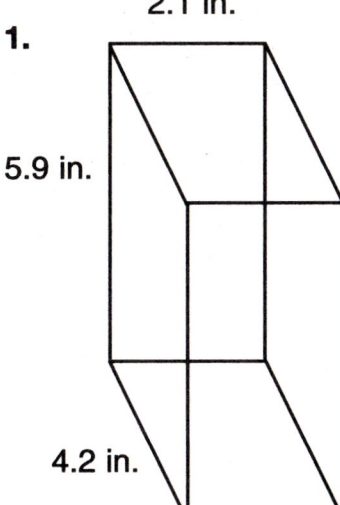

2. 5.1 in., 2.8 in., 3.1 in.
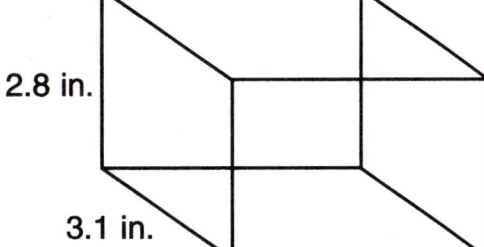

3. 4.1 in., 4.1 in., 4.1 in.
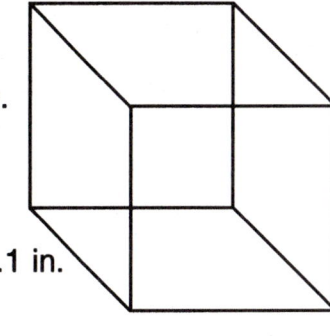

152 Around or Across

Using the formulas $C = \pi d$ and $\pi \approx 3.14$, choose the reasonable estimate of the circumference or the diameter for each object.

1. A compact disk has a diameter of 12 cm. Its circumference is
    a. 38 cm   b. 3.8 cm

2. A can of stew measures 31 cm around. Its diameter is
    a. 100 cm   b. 10 cm

3. A toy truck wheel is 25 cm around. Its diameter is
    a. 78 cm   b. 8 cm

153 Percent Grids

Estimate the percent that is shaded of each bar.

1. 2.  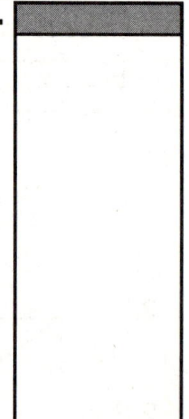 3. 4.

Fraction Tic-Tac-Two   154

Use estimation and number sense to determine which row, column, or diagonal has a sum of 2.

1.

$\frac{3}{4}$	$\frac{2}{3}$	$1\frac{1}{3}$
$\frac{1}{2}$	$\frac{1}{2}$	$\frac{1}{10}$
$1\frac{1}{4}$	$\frac{1}{4}$	$\frac{1}{2}$

2.

$\frac{2}{3}$	$\frac{1}{2}$	$\frac{11}{12}$
$\frac{7}{12}$	$\frac{1}{6}$	$\frac{2}{3}$
$\frac{1}{2}$	$\frac{7}{12}$	$1\frac{1}{6}$

Fractions at the Mall   155

1. Sean bought a $19.95 CD on sale for $5.00 off. The discount is approximately what fraction of the original price? The sale price is approximately what fraction of the original price?

2. A $149.95 jacket is sale priced at $99.95. The ad stated that the jackets are $\frac{1}{3}$ off. Is it correctly priced? Explain.

Clustering III   156

The addends in each problem are "clustered" around a number. Find the product of that number and the number of addends to estimate each sum.

1. $8.756 + 9.231 + 8.99 + 9.001 + 8.761 \approx$

2. $3.923 + 4.192 + 4.204 + 3.776 + 4.011 \approx$

157 Formulate

Round the quantities and use the formulas to estimate the answers.

1. Paige drove 91 mi. from Omaha to Lincoln at an average of 62 mph. How long did it take? ($d = rt$)
2. Find the area of a triangular kite with a base of $3\frac{1}{6}$ ft. and a height of $7\frac{5}{6}$ ft. ($A = \frac{1}{2}bh$).
3. It took Duane $5\frac{1}{4}$ hours to drive round-trip from his home to Pierre, South Dakota, 151 miles each way. Find his average rate of travel.

158 Decimal Tic-Tac-Toe

Use estimation and number sense to determine which row, column, or diagonal has a sum of 1.

1.

0.25	0.67	0.25
0.5	0.3	0.1
0.8	0.25	0.45

2.

0.7	0.5	0.4
0.2	0.25	0.67
0.2	0.35	0.45

Clean-Up! 159

1. The 20-oz. size of Super-Clean-It is 99¢. The 30-oz. size is $1.42. Which is the better buy?
2. You have a 20¢-off coupon for each size of Super-Clean-It. Which is the better buy if you use the coupon?

Fundraiser Fun 160

The Student Council is selling fun-time movie passes to raise money for the annual field day. Printing the passes costs $22. The materials for the field day cost $295. If the profit from each pass is about 95¢, approximately how many passes must be sold to break even?

    a. 285   b. 300   c. 335   d. 400

C and P 161

Compare the circumference of a circle 10" in diameter to the perimeter of a square 10" on each side.

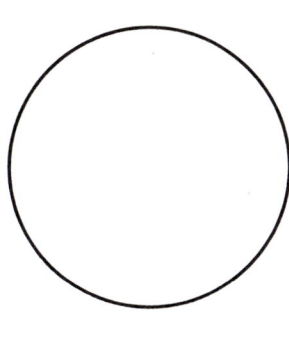

$C = \pi d$
$P = 4s$

162 Room Designs

Give reasonable estimates for the dimensions of the pieces of furniture labeled in the diagram. Each grid square represents 4 sq. ft.

Bed _____ x _____   Chest _____ x _____
Desk _____ x _____   Chair _____ x _____
Nightstand _____ x _____   Stool _____ x _____

163 Decimal Tic-Tac-Two

Use estimation and number sense to determine which row, column, or diagonal has a sum of 2.

1.

1.2	0.67	0.23
0.6	0.3	1.1
0.8	1.25	0.15

2.

0.7	0.5	0.55
0.2	0.25	1.67
1.2	1.35	0.45

Number Sense 164

Determine the correct answer choice without actually performing the operation. Consider the place values, number of digits in the problems, etc.

1. 2,446 + 432 + 9,812 =   a. 1,190   b. 12,690   c. 11,690
2. 6,264 − 3,812 =   a. 2,452   b. 3,452   c. 2,456
3. 233 x 43 =   a. 10,016   b. 1,019   c. 10,019
4. 3600 ÷ 60 =   a. 6   b. 60   c. 600

Don't Solve These 165

Without solving each problem, determine whether the missing number (?) is greater than or less than the underlined number.

1. $\frac{4}{5}$ x 20 = ?
2. $1\frac{2}{3}$ x $\frac{3}{4}$ = ?
3. 1.5 x 30 = ?
4. 0.5 x 1.5 = ?
5. ? ÷ 36 = $1\frac{3}{4}$
6. ? ÷ 24 = $\frac{1}{4}$
7. ? ÷ 25 = 0.75
8. ? ÷ 45 = 1.5

Digital Solutions 166

How many digits are in each answer?

1. 732 + 523
2. 499 + 299
3. 4567 − 4321
4. 6789 − 2345
5. 23 x 34
6. 26 x 86
7. 4500 ÷ 300
8. 4500 ÷ 5

167 Fraction Mismatch

Three of the four fractions in each row are equivalent. Use number sense and estimation to determine the fraction that does not match.

1. $\frac{24}{36}$ $\frac{32}{48}$ $\frac{50}{45}$ $\frac{12}{18}$
2. $\frac{46}{92}$ $\frac{51}{102}$ $\frac{75}{150}$ $\frac{54}{60}$
3. $\frac{45}{27}$ $\frac{50}{60}$ $\frac{100}{60}$ $\frac{15}{9}$
4. $\frac{12}{18}$ $\frac{33}{22}$ $\frac{90}{60}$ $\frac{36}{24}$

168 Exercise Schedule

Olivia hopes to exercise 45 minutes every other day. Her trainer suggested the following workout. Can Olivia do the workout in 45 minutes?

stretch—5 mins.
run—two 12-minute mi. on a treadmill
lift light weights—$7\frac{1}{2}$ mins.
use stepper—4 mins. 45 secs.
do cool down stretches—5.5 mins.

169 Quick Estimate—Fractions IV

1. Which is the best estimate for $6\frac{2}{3} \times 2\frac{2}{9}$?   12   15   21

2. Which is the best estimate for $6\frac{2}{3} \div 2\frac{2}{9}$?   3   4   5

Common-Sense Percents 170

Decide if each statement is sense or nonsense. Explain.

1. The Liberty High Lions won 125% of their games.
2. Joe correctly answered 45 of 50 questions. His grade was 90%.
3. Jacob averaged his grades of 81%, 82%, 86%, 91% to be 90%.
4. Cassandra paid $3.00 sales tax for a $6.00 purchase.
5. For lunch, 50% of the class ordered sandwiches, 50% of the class ordered salad, 50% of the class ordered French fries, and 50% of the class ordered juice.

Compared to 500 171

State whether each quantity is greater than or less than 500.

1. number of students in your school
2. number of minutes in a day
3. number of dimes in $20.00
4. number of cars in your town
5. number of feet in a mile

Percent Benchmarks II 172

Benchmarks			
$25\% = \frac{1}{4}$	$50\% = \frac{1}{2}$	$75\% = \frac{3}{4}$	$100\% = 1$

1. Which is the best estimate for 27% of 48?   1.5   9.6   13
2. Which is the best estimate for 73% of 80?   6   60   72

173 Decimal Match

Each problem in the first column has the same answer as a problem in the second column. Estimate the solutions to determine the matches.

1. 7.6 + 2 .5
2. 10.6 – 2. 2
3. 9.6 – 1.75
4. 4.7 + 4.7

a. 6.2 + 2.2
b. 2.15 + 7.25
c. 5.2 + 4.9
d. 8.5 – 0.65

174 Quick Estimate–Angles III

Estimate the measure of the angle. Circle the correct answer.

55°   85°   95°   125°

175 Clean-Up II

Clean-Up Detergent comes in two sizes. The 40-oz. size costs $3.89 and the 2-qt. size costs $6.49. Which is the better buy?

Area Estimates 176

If the area of the square is 16 square inches, estimate the area of each region. (Hint: $A = 4s$)

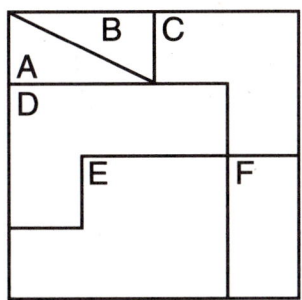

Wood Shop 177

To complete a woodworking project, Natalie needs pieces of wood in these lengths: $\frac{2}{3}$ ft., $\frac{2}{3}$ yd., 6 in., $1\frac{1}{2}$ ft., and $\frac{1}{4}$ yd. Can she cut all the strips from a piece of wood 6 ft. long?

Powerful Numbers 178

An *exponent* tells you how many times a number is a factor.

Example: $2^3 = 2 \times 2 \times 2$ or 8 $3^4 = 3 \times 3 \times 3 \times 3$ or 81

Which is greater?

1. 3^2 or 2^4
2. 5^3 or 6^2
3. 3^3 or 5^2

179 Check the Data

Make a line graph of the data.

Time (days)	Height (cm)
2	2
4	5
6	9
8	14
10	20

Height
Time

Estimate the height on day 3 _____; on day 7 _____; on day 9 _____.

180 The "Round Table" III

Complete the table by rounding each number to the indicated place value.

Number	Ones	Tenths	Hundreths	Thousandths
1. 3.6455				
2. 5.5039				
3. 9.8765				
4. 12.3456				
5. 0.70605				

ANSWER KEY

Activity 1
Yes (4 x $3 = $12).

Activity 2
1. 4
2. 4
3. 5

Activity 3
1. b
2. c

Activity 4
1. 0.0242   5. 1.536   9. 10.854
2. 1.815   6. 75.9   10. 5.3667
3. 0.0055   7. 72.82   11. 0.0588
4. 1.02   8. 64.842 12. 0.82

Activity 5
|__B__D_E_C____|__A_____|
0              $\frac{1}{2}$ 1

Activity 6
Answer depends on size of class.

Activity 7
1. Answer depends on size of class.
2. ≈ $6

Activity 8
Answer depends on size of class.

Activity 9

Number	2	3	4	5	6	9
1. 15,480	y	y	y	y	y	y
2. 34,650	y	y		y	y	y
3. 75,400	y		y	y		
4. 99,999		y				y
5. 1,000	y		y	y		

Activity 10
1. b
2. c

Activity 11
1. estimate   3. exact
2. exact   4. estimate

Activity 12
111

Activity 13
≈ 1550

Activity 14
1. short sleeves
2. 5°C
3. degrees Fahrenheit

Activity 15
1. b
2. b

Activity 16
1. $39
2. $38.50
3. The second figure is closer because rounding to the nearest 10¢ is rounding by a smaller piece of the whole.

Activity 17
1. b
2. a

Activity 18
25°

Activity 19
A. 12 sq. in.   C. 16 sq. in.
B. 4 sq. in.   D. 32 sq. in.

Activity 20
1. 12 secs.
2. 47 mins., 300 mi.

Activity 21
1. 1   3. $\frac{1}{2}$ 5. 0   7. $\frac{1}{2}$
2. 0   4. $\frac{3}{4}$ 6. $\frac{3}{4}$ 8. 1

Activity 22
No. The minimum weight is 87 oz.; 5 lb. = 80 oz.

Activity 23
1. c
2. a

Activity 24
Answers may include: Jenny jogged at a constant speed before stopping for awhile. She then ran faster at a constant speed. She stopped jogging.

Activity 25
1. $\frac{1}{2} + 1\frac{1}{2} + 2 = 4$
2. $2 + 0 + \frac{1}{2} = 2\frac{1}{2}$
3. $\frac{1}{2} + 2 + 0 = 2\frac{1}{2}$
4. $\frac{1}{2} + 1 + 1\frac{1}{2} = 3$

Activity 26

Number	Thousands	Hundreds	Tens
1. 3,455	3,000	3,500	3,460
2. 2,503	3,000	2,500	2,500
3. 98,765	99,000	98,800	98,770
4. 123,456	123,000	123,500	123,460
5. 70,605	71,000	70,600	70,610

Activity 27
1. 23.92
5. 1.11
6. 15.4

Activity 28
Answers will vary. "Shoe units" vary because people wear different sizes of shoes.

Activity 29
1. $1 + 1 + 2 + \frac{1}{2} + 2 + 0 = 6\frac{1}{2}$
2. $(2 + 2) - (1 + \frac{1}{2}) - (1 + 1) = \frac{1}{2}$
3. $2 - (1 - \frac{1}{2}) - (\frac{1}{2} - 0) = 1$

Activity 30
Answers will vary.

Activity 31
$7\frac{1}{2}$ lb., or 7 lb. to the nearest pound.

Activity 32
1. 2,335–2,344
2. 56,650–56,749
3. 13,500–14,499
4. 13,950–14,049
5. 13,995–14,004

Activity 33
1. b
2. a

Activity 34
Yes.

Activity 35

Num.	Tens	Ones	Tenths	Hund.
1. 34.551	30	35	34.6	34.55
2. 7.513	10	8	7.5	7.51
3. 108.765	110	109	108.8	108.77
4. 2.345	0	2	2.3	2.35
5. 70.605	70	71	70.6	70.61

Activity 36
1. b
2. a

Activity 37
1. 90
2. 9 times the middle number.
3. 108

Activity 38
≈ $440

Activity 39
7 yd.

Activity 40
1. $\frac{1}{2}$ 3. $\frac{1}{2}$ 5. 0   7. 1
2. $\frac{3}{4}$ 4. $\frac{1}{4}$ 6. $\frac{1}{2}$ 8. $\frac{1}{4}$

Activity 41
1. 1.5 km
2. 22°C

Activity 42
1. $\frac{1}{4}$ 3. $\frac{1}{6}$ 5. $\frac{1}{6}$
2. $\frac{1}{4}$ 4. $\frac{1}{12}$ 6. $\frac{1}{12}$

Activity 43
1. 200 mL   3. 35 g
2. 50 g   4. 100 mL

Activity 44
Answers will vary.

Activity 45
$16.50

Activity 46
Yes.

Activity 47
1. $\frac{1}{3}$ 3. $\frac{5}{6}$
2. $\frac{1}{2}$ 4. $\frac{1}{3}$ to $\frac{2}{5}$

Activity 48
1. ≈ 6 gal.
2. ≈ $9

ANSWER KEY

Activity 49
A—3 sq. ft.   D—8 sq. ft.
B—2 sq. ft.   E—3 sq. ft.
C—$4\frac{1}{2}$ sq. ft.

Activity 50
85°

Activity 51
A $3\frac{3}{4}$ D $2\frac{1}{4}$
B $\frac{7}{8}$ E $4\frac{1}{8}$
C $1\frac{1}{2}$

Activity 52
A 6.5   D 9.5
B 8   E 10.5
C 2.5

Activity 53
1. c   3. b
2. c   4. c

Activity 54
1. 220   3. 132
2. 55   4. 176

Activity 55
Yes, it will make 15 cups.

Activity 56
≈ $17.50

Activity 57
at Ed's for 1 hr. to 15 hrs.; at Dontae's for 15 hrs. to 20 hrs.

Activity 58
1. b   4. e
2. d   5. a
3. c

Activity 59
Yes, for ≈ $144.50.

Activity 60
1. c   3. c
2. b   4. Answers will vary.

Activity 61
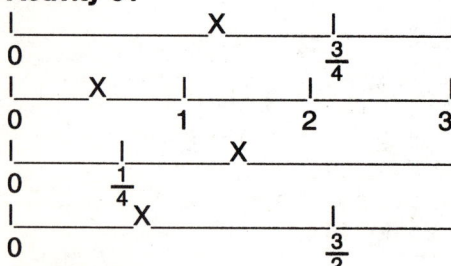

Activity 62
more than $300

Activity 63
13–21 lb.

Activity 64
red, $\frac{1}{6}$; black, $\frac{1}{6}$; blue, $\frac{1}{4}$;
green, $\frac{1}{12}$; yellow, $\frac{1}{3}$

Activity 65
1. $\frac{4}{25}$ 2. $\frac{9}{100}$ 4. $\frac{9}{16}$ 5. $2\frac{1}{4}$
Mike didn't multiply the denominators.

Activity 66
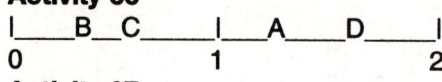

Activity 67
$\frac{1}{2}$ hr.—30 mi. $2\frac{1}{2}$ hrs.—110 mi.
1 hr.—50 mi.   3 hrs.—120 mi.
$1\frac{1}{2}$ hrs.—60 mi. $3\frac{1}{2}$ hrs.—145 mi.
2 hrs.—90 mi.

Activity 68
1. 24
2. 45
3. $90

Activity 69
a.

Activity 70
1. 90%   2. 15%   3. 60%
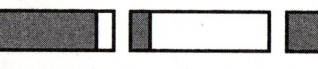

Activity 71
96 sq. in.

Activity 72
1. $1\frac{1}{2} - 0 - \frac{1}{2} = 1$
2. $2 - 0 - \frac{1}{2} = 1\frac{1}{2}$
3. $2 - 1 - \frac{1}{2} = \frac{1}{2}$
4. $1 - 0 - \frac{1}{2} = \frac{1}{2}$

Activity 73
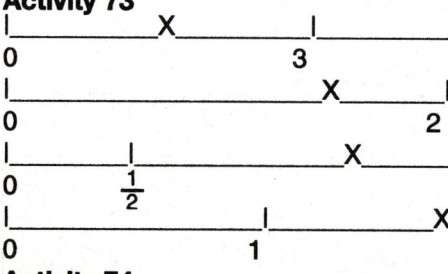

Activity 74
1. c   3. d
2. a   4. b

Activity 75
1. varies
2. greater than 500
3. less than 500
4. varies
5. greater than 500

Activity 76
1. 4   3. 4   5. 4   7. 3
2. 5   4. 3   6. 5   8. 2

Activity 77
≈ 8:20

Activity 78
30 hrs. ≈ $360;
6 hrs. on holiday ≈ $144

Activity 79
1. 240   3. 560
2. 360   4. 450

Activity 80
1. $\frac{2}{3}$ 4. $\frac{4}{5}$
2. $\frac{8}{9}$ 5. 0.022
3. $\frac{6}{11}$

Activity 81
Answers will vary.

Activity 82
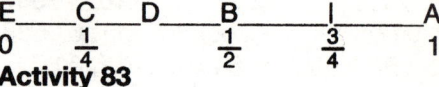

Activity 83
b

Activity 84
c

Activity 85
$C \approx \pi 24$; $P \approx 32$. Therefore the circumference ≈ $\frac{3}{4}$ of the perimeter.

Activity 86
c

Activity 87
1 to 3

Activity 88
1. $21.00
2. $21.50

Activity 89
15°C ≈ 60°F
30°C ≈ 90°F
35°C ≈ 100°F

Activity 90
|___C_____B_|__D___A__|
0   1   2

Activity 91
380 mi.

Activity 92
set a $\frac{9}{10}$ set c $\frac{2}{3}$
set b $\frac{15}{35}$ set d $\frac{2}{4}$

Activity 93
1. 2 L   4. 300 mL
2. cube   5. 80 L
3. 15 gal.

Activity 94
Cecil's Cycles

Activity 95
1. 91 cm   4. 120 m
2. 21.5 cm   5. 1 mm
3. 30 mm

Activity 96
1. $\frac{1}{2} + 1 + 1\frac{1}{2} = 3$ 3. $\frac{1}{2} \times 2 = 1$
2. $2 - 0 - \frac{1}{2} = 1\frac{1}{2}$ 4. $1 \div 2 = \frac{1}{2}$

Activity 97
1. $4.50   2. $6.60   3. $13.50

ANSWER KEY

Activity 98
1. $18.20   3. $25.00
2. $11.00   4. $4.80

Activity 99
1. $\frac{44}{45}$ 2. 0.91   3. 0.67

Activity 100
apple—120°; blueberry—45°;
cherry—90°; pecan—45°
peach—60°

Activity 101
1. round up (to be sure to have enough paint)
2. round down (can't put in part of a can)
3. round down (don't want to go over the weight)

Activity 102
1. 28 ÷ 7 = 4   3. 48 ÷ 6 = 8
2. 50 ÷ 5 = 10   4. 35 ÷ 7 = 5

Activity 103
1. c
2. b

Activity 104
Stories will vary—should include stopping from 7:10–7:20 and 7:40–7:50 and returning home before 8:00.

Activity 105
1. a   3. c
2. b   4. a

Activity 106
Stories will vary; should include
1. running at constant speed;
2. running faster;
3. stopping;
4. running slower than from 3:45 to 4:00.

Activity 107
19% or ≈ 20%

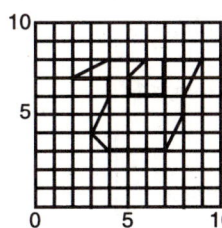

Activity 108
Yes.

Activity 109
1. 4 tokens
2. 5 trips
3. 2 eggs
You will have 2 tokens left over—you can't use them all and divide them evenly; the ferry won't be full every trip because you have 2 too many cars to make all full trips; you will have 2 too many eggs to fill cartons of 12.

Activity 110
1. Answers will vary
2. ≈ 6 hrs.

Activity 111
1.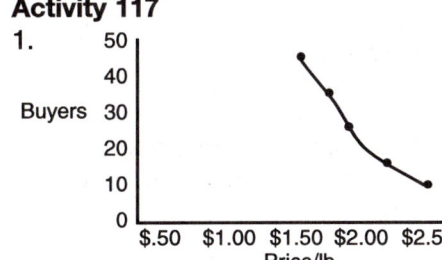

2. ≈ 650   3. ≈ 400   4. ≈ 200

Activity 112
1. ≈ 8 × (5 + $\frac{1}{4}$) = (8 × 5) + (8 × $\frac{1}{4}$) = 40 + 2 = 42
2. ≈ 9 × (6 + $\frac{1}{3}$) = (9 × 6) + (9 × $\frac{1}{3}$) = 54 + 3 = 57
3. ≈ 12 × (3 + $\frac{5}{6}$) = (12 × 3) + (12 × $\frac{5}{6}$) = 36 + 10 = 46

Activity 113
2. $1\frac{3}{7}$ 4. $\frac{1}{10}$ 5. $9\frac{5}{12}$

Activity 114
1. b
2. c

Activity 115
border ≈ 44 ft.
carpet ≈ 120 sq. ft.

Activity 116
1. a   4. a
2. b   5. c
3. b

Activity 117
1. [graph]

2. ≈ 40; ≈ 20; ≈ 8

Activity 118
1.–3. Answers will vary.
4. 100%
5. 0%
6.–7. Answers will vary.

Activity 119
1. ≈ 60 cal.
2. 1 hr.

Activity 120
1. b
2. c

Activity 121
1. A $\frac{1}{2}$; B $\frac{1}{4}$; C $\frac{1}{12}$; D $\frac{1}{6}$
2. A $\frac{3}{8}$; B $\frac{1}{8}$; C $\frac{1}{8}$; D $\frac{3}{8}$

Activity 122
1. 72
2. 128

Activity 123
c

Activity 124
No, she needs 9 hrs. 15 mins. total.

Activity 125
b

Activity 126
1. ≈ 164°; ≈ 188°   4. ≈ 73°; ≈ 91°
2. ≈ 102°; ≈ 148°   5. ≈ 69°; ≈ 77°
3. ≈ 81°; ≈ 115°   6. ≈ 68°; ≈ 70°

Activity 127
400 lb.

Activity 128
1. ft.   5. gal.
2. in. or ft.   6. ft.
3. qt.   7. ft. or yd.
4. sq. ft. or sq. yd. 8. in.

Activity 129
No, he needs 8.75 inches total.

Activity 130
1. C ≈ 62 in.; A ≈ 314 sq. in.
2. b, f

Activity 131
1.–2. Answers depend on items selected.

Activity 132
1. Yes, there's a $1 price advantage at Furniture Clearance.
2. No, the sale prices would be the same.

Activity 133
1. 350°F   3. 40°F
2. 25°C   4. 20°F

Activity 134
d

Activity 135
1. 38 ≈ 19d, d ≈ 2
2. 25/w ≈ 5, w ≈ 5
3. 62 ≈ 31x, x ≈ 2

Activity 136
Answers will vary with the individuals.

Activity 137
1. 55°F
2. 67°F

Activity 138
1. 15°C
2. 20°C

Activity 139
1. $\frac{7}{16}$
2. $\frac{1}{2}$
Dakota should choose 2.

ANSWER KEY

Activity 140
Answers will vary.
Activity 141
b
Activity 142
1. $4\frac{3}{4}$ in.
2. 9–10 hrs.
Activity 143
1. c
2. d
Activity 144
Estimated Miles
Mercury 31,000,000
Venus 62,000,000
Earth 93,000,000
Mars 139,500,000
Jupiter 465,000,000
Saturn 852,500,000
Activity 145
1. 20 lb.   4. 150 lb.
2. 12 lb.   5. 1 lb.
3. 252 lb.
Activity 146
1. $125
2. $70
Activity 147
1. $x \approx 3$
2. $w \approx 8$
3. $y \approx 6$
Activity 148
1. What was his average speed?
2. How much gas did he buy?
3. How many miles per gallon did he average?
Activity 149
1. 66 sq. in.
2. 28 sq. in.
Activity 150
figure 1. second row
figure 2. diagonal, lower left to upper right
Activity 151
1. 48 cu. in.
2. 45 cu. in.
3. 64 cu. in.—holds the most
Activity 152
1. a
2. b
3. b
Activity 153
1. 25%   3. 10%
2. 75%   4. 80%
Activity 154
1. third row
2. diagonal, upper left to lower right

Activity 155
1. $\frac{1}{4}$; $\frac{3}{4}$
2. Yes; $149.95 ≈ $150; $\frac{1}{3}$ of $150 is $50; $150 minus $50 = $100 ≈ $99.95.
Activity 156
1. 9 x 5 = 45
2. 4 x 5 = 20
Activity 157
1. $1\frac{1}{2}$ hrs.
2. 12 sq. ft.
3. 60 mph
Activity 158
1. diagonal, upper left to lower right
2. third row
Activity 159
1. 30-oz.
2. 20-oz.
Activity 160
c
Activity 161
3 to 4; C ≈ 30 in., P ≈ 40 in.
Activity 162
Bed: 6' x 7'   Chest 2' x 3'
Desk: 3' x 4'   Chair 2' x 2'
Nightstand: 1' x 2' Stool: 1' x 1'
Activity 163
1. second row
2. diagonal, lower left to upper right
Activity 164
1. b   3. c
2. a   4. b
Activity 165
1. less than   5. greater than
2. greater than   6. less than
3. greater than   7. less than
4. less than   8. greater than
Activity 166
1. 4   3. 3   5. 3   7. 2
2. 3   4. 4   6. 4   8. 3
Activity 167
1. $\frac{50}{45}$ 3. $\frac{50}{60}$
2. $\frac{54}{60}$ 4. $\frac{12}{18}$
Activity 168
No, the proposed workout would take about 50 minutes.
Activity 169
1. 15
2. 3
Activity 170
1. nonsense—couldn't win more games than they played
2. sense

3. nonsense—only 1 of 4 grades was barely over 90% and the rest were well below, so the grades couldn't average that high.
4. nonsense—would mean the sales tax was 50% of the price
5. sense
Activity 171
1. Answers will vary according to the school.
2. greater than
3. less than
4. Answers will vary; students probably have enough information to only guess.
5. greater than
Activity 172
1. 13
2. 60
Activity 173
1. c   3. d
2. a   4. b
Activity 174
125°
Activity 175
40-oz.
Activity 176
A 1 sq. in.   D 4 sq. in.
B 1 sq. in.   E 5 sq. in.
C 3 sq. in.   F 2 sq. in.
Activity 177
Yes; needs about 69" and has 72"
Activity 178
1. 2^4
2. 5^3
3. 3^3
Activity 179

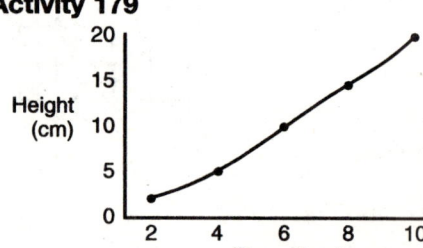

day 3—4 cm
day 7—12 cm
day 9—17 cm
Activity 180

Num.	Ones	Tenths	Hund.	Thous.
1. 3.6455	4	3.6	3.65	3.646
2. 5.5039	6	5.5	5.50	5.504
3. 9.8765	10	9.9	9.88	9.877
4. 12.3456	12	12.3	12.35	12.346
5. 0.70605	1	0.7	0.71	0.706